Praise

"Reading Ginny Andrews's *Good Talk...Good Talk* is a lot like hanging out with that girlfriend that invariably makes you laugh until you cry. She's just a little off color and says out loud the words you think but are too chicken to speak. She's totally relatable in sharing tales of the human condition – in all its craziness, and her kind heart comes through even when her wit is at its sharpest. Whether you take Good Talk...one talk at a time or tackle it all in one sitting when you feel like no one understands you, this book will bring a smile to your face and remind you that you are not alone in feeling like the most awkward person on the planet."

Lauren Cassel Brownell, Author of *Zen and the Art of Housekeeping* and *Dying to Donate*

"*Good Talk...Good Talk* is a laugh out loud winner, filled with quirky stories reminiscent of Patrick McManus. It'll have you chuckling and looking for creative ways to tell your own family tales. Andrews paints pictures of salt of the earth people and 'not so everyday life' that make the reader realize maybe their lives and families are a little more normal than they first thought."

J. Andersen, author of *The Breeding Tree,*
The Gene Rift, and *Legacy's Impact*

Good Talk...Good Talk

Ginny Andrews

Ginny Andrews Comedy, LLC

ginnyandrewscomedy.com

ISBN: 979-8-9884199-1-4 (paperback)

979-8-9884199-0-7 (eBook)

For my parents, thank you for putting up with my weirdness all these years. Your love and support have no limits, and I don't have the words to truly thank you. I love you with all my heart.

Food for Thought

There is a good amount of ass in this book. I can assure you; no donkeys or horses were harmed in the making of this book. In fact, they were given a crap ton of treats, and even some Little Debbie Cakes (not on purpose; I wanted to eat those!). After two photo shoots with Racket (the star of the show), he and I had a hard time choosing the best pictures.

I had ones I liked, but he insisted on the ones that made his ass look good! Therefore, the final product includes an overwhelming amount of donkey pictures throughout. Don't read too much into this. In fact, just sit back and enjoy the circus that is my life! "Good Talk...Good Talk!"

Sincerely,

Ginny & Racket

Contents

Note from the Author

I loathe confrontation. I can practice my speech repeatedly, but it never happens to play out in real life like it does in my head. Nor do I get to say page nine, addendum A, of my thoroughly planned out notes. Instead, I end up walking away with the words, **"Good Talk...Good Talk,"** echoing in my mind as well as some major stomach issues!

This book is for all the awkward weirdos out there— like me! The people who feel like Walter Mitty: that the best moments in their life, and the best things they say, all happen in their head.

You can find me out on a date with a guy who face-plants in his food and inhales it like it's cocaine. Or at the doctor's office trying to figure out if the gown for my latest visit fastens in the front or the back because I'm not quite sure what kind of visit this will be. Plus, the holes. The holes in the gown always get me. They should really specify which body part goes in what hole ahead of time.

This is me. I have a hidden talent—I can make any moment and any situation awkward. Approaching my forties head on (ugh, even typing that makes me need to breathe heavily into a paper bag), I can't hide it or make excuses for it anymore. I am who I am.

In my younger years, I was too racy for the church crowd but too much of a goody-goody for the bar scene. As I have gotten older, I have realized I don't adult well. I am not intellectually stimulating enough for the book club goers; I don't have a husband or kid to hang out with the couples' crowd. The bar rats are now alcoholics, and my potty mouth still gets me in trouble with my small group at church. Where does that leave this gangsta?

I am a former high school and college public speaking teacher with a speech impediment, a wannabe writer who struggles with writing in complete sentences, and an aspiring comedian with social anxiety. This shit just got real! I'm ready to embrace it and help you find your awkward, non-fitting-in, tired-of-apologizing-for-who-you-are voice. To quote Coolio, "Come along and ride on a fantastic voyage...slide, slide, slippity-slide."

Life can be amazing one moment, and the next moment you find out you have cancer. However, after a year's worth of treatment you are in remission, but then you die in a car accident. Life is unpredictable. If we don't find a way to laugh through the ironic moments, or at least embrace Alanis Morissette, we aren't going to be able to enjoy the best moments in life—the ones where all we can say is, "**Good Talk...Good Talk!**"

Chapter 1

Self-Realization

I was driving down a busy highway and I saw a sign that said, "Self-Realization Fellowship." This is awesome and exactly what I need! My self realizes I have a ton of issues and maybe they can fix them!

I walked into the bookstore and asked for some information on how to get started fixing my issues. The nice lady pointed me to a shelf full of pamphlets and books titled "free literature."

I love free things. The world loves free things—especially Oprah's audience members. For example, once in my hometown they were offering free snow cones at the local Hawaiian ice shop. The line was backed up around four blocks, causing traffic jams on the loop (our small-town version of an interstate) all to get a free cup of flavored frozen water. You could find me waiting in line with the rest of the town. Afterward, I realized the amount of gas I used ended up costing more than walking into the store and paying for a damn snow cone!

I stuffed several brochures in my bag, along with a handout on quotes from Gandhi (by the way, this homie is remarkable). Can you imagine getting to have a therapy session with the big G? I asked the nice lady if I could make a donation for all the information she was so generously giving me, and she kindly smiled back at me and replied, "No need, my child, just enjoy and find peace." I think she could tell by my anxious, neurotic personality I could use all the help I could get!

I walked out of the office beaming with a newfound sense of hope. What a nice lady and a peaceful place.

After reading through all the "free literature," I was hooked. This stuff just made sense. Now it was time to get started! The biggest tool I picked up in my readings was to meditate, and their suggestion was to accomplish a meditative state through yoga. This could be a problem.

In the last yoga class I attended, I was asked to leave and return the yoga mat I borrowed. I thought it was free, but apparently not. This time was going to be different. I was driven. I had a purpose. I wasn't just trying to get a body like Jennifer Aniston. I was on a religious journey to find peace, or at least cure the sciatica that was rocking my back.

I walked cautiously into the yoga studio with my mat in hand. Yes, I purchased my own mat; I was serious this time! Well, I didn't exactly purchase it. The Sports Authority down the road from the yoga studio was offering free yoga mats with the purchase of a pair of Sanuk sandals. I purchased the sandals, returned them, and secretly kept my mat. I know, I'm a bad person...but this was before my religious journey so I can't be held accountable for my actions quite yet.

The woman leading the class looked like a modern-day hippie, and she seemed to be a peaceful person. This was a good sign, and I felt like she could be my guide into my meditative state of bliss. This time was going to be different. This time I was here to find peace and get in touch with God. This was religious yoga, not fitness yoga; therefore no one could judge my lack of athletic ability in this place of tranquility.

I noticed the room was insanely hot. Maybe they'd forgotten to pay their electric bill too. I had been showering and hanging out at my neighbor's for the past week since I forgot to pay mine.

I positioned myself in the back, the very back so that no one would be behind me when my ass was in a compromising position! We started off by doing some deep breathing and stretching. I liked the stretching, but breathing in a hot room full of strangers was a bit odd, and some of these strangers sounded like they had COPD.

Next, we focused on deep poses named after animals: dog, cobra, butterfly, and peacock...or at least I think she said peacock. It was hard to hear above the deep wheezing and Enya music. While in my downward-facing dog stance, I looked around and noticed my downward dog looked more like a cat going poop in a litter box in comparison to the rest of the crew in the room.

It was hard to focus on getting into a meditative state, where one finds peace and gets closer to God, when I kept losing my balance, falling over, and hitting my neighbors on both sides of me. Needless to say, balance was a problem for me.

Problem number two, other than the fact that I was about to have a heat stroke, was flexibility, or lack thereof. I'm about as flexible as a piece of wood. When I was a cheerleader in junior high, I was a flyer, only because I weighed eighty pounds, not due to my amazing toe touches. My cheer sponsor told me to clap when I was at the top since I couldn't stretch out my leg on my toe extend. It was more like a squished-up, bent knee with a toe grab.

Given all my flexibility issues, I decided to start off by modifying the stretches. If I tried to bend like both of my neighbors, I would be taken out of the class on a stretcher! After stretch number ten that I couldn't do, I began to get frustrated. Instead of focusing on breathing deep into my stretch, letting everything go, and relaxing, I had to focus on controlling my breathing so I wouldn't pass out from the heat, lose my balance and hit my neighbors again, or fart. I was holding in a fart per minute, because when I get stressed, anxious, nervous, or even excited—I get the farts.

How was this peaceful? How was I supposed to focus on communicating with God and meditating with all these other things going on? How in the world did these people's bodies bend like that? I felt like I was in a Kama Sutra class. I mean, I don't know what that is really. I saw some videos on YouTube by accident and decided I wouldn't sign up for that extracurricular activity anytime soon.

The instructor said, "Let it all go" over and over, so that is exactly what I did! I let go, fell backward, hit the back wall, knocked over the rack of weights (which came rolling across the floor like hand grenades), and completely disturbed the ambiance of the class!

Everyone started to scream and panic, even the peaceful hippie instructor, and I finally was able to let go...a fart (that I had been holding in for an hour) and some major curse words! The instructor gave me a look that implied, "Please don't ever come back!" Wow, leave it to me to make even a peaceful hippie angry.

I frantically grabbed all my stuff (I mean, I couldn't leave my mat behind, it was expensive) and I ran out the door with my tail tucked between my legs. Instead of finding God, peace, and tranquility, I'd added more issues to my list of issues.

I now knew I couldn't do yoga, or meditate, or at least I couldn't meditate while doing yoga. However, I'm a fighter, and I decided not to give up on the meditation thing. Maybe I could actually calm down, find peace, de-stress, lower my anxiety, and bring myself closer to God through meditation if not trying to balance on my head or in a position named after an animal. Let's do this.

I arrived home, turned out all the lights, and placed myself in a comfortable position in the middle of my bedroom. The shades were drawn, the box fan was on high to help block out noise and my hot flashes, and my phone and headphones were beside me. I went to YouTube and typed in "anxiety reducing meditation."

There were tons of videos that pulled up, and I found myself getting anxious deciding which video to choose to make me less anxious. I finally decided on one by a Michael Sealey. He seemed to have a ton of videos posted on meditation, so he must be the "meditation guru."

I pressed play and I immediately liked his voice. I started to wonder if he was single and then I pressed pause to look at his picture. Wow, a good face to go along with that voice. I then realized I was off task, so I popped myself in the head and got back to work. He told me to relax, take deep breaths, blank out my mind, and I was trying so hard and doing awesome—then I had to pee.

After I came back from the bathroom, I was serious. No more interruptions. I resumed the video. Again, he told me to breathe (man that's a lot of breathing) and to close my eyes and imagine a peaceful place. I tried to get there, and then I realized the cross-legged position was hurting my bum knee.

I decided to stretch out my legs, even though that was breaking the meditation rules based on all my research (I'd Googled meditation positions). My mind began to wander, and I noticed that not only did my knee hurt, but so did my back and neck.

I pressed pause and immediately went to make a chiropractor appointment, but I hurried back and resumed the video. We were back on the breathing. I tried to take deep breaths, and then he told me to imagine a beach and to listen to the waves rolling in with the tide. He asked me what I heard. What did I hear? A garbage truck and the dog started barking, so I had to let her out.

After I let the dog out, I hurried back to my meditating position and resumed the video. He was telling me to relax and go deeper into that happy place. What if I never found that happy place? How did I go deeper if I wasn't there? Shit, I was so messing up. I gave myself a couple of pops to the head and told myself to focus.

Okay, I am there. I'm on the beach. Wait, did I put on sunscreen? Where is my towel? I reminded myself I wouldn't get too much UV exposure from the lights being out.

He told me to go deeper into that tranquil place. I tried so hard to stay in the moment, but by doing so, I squished up my nose, and I had a grimaced look on my face as though I was in pain. I'm pretty sure Gandhi didn't look like he was constipated when meditating.

Michael began to count and said after each number I should go deeper and deeper into a relaxed state. One...two...three...

When he got to ten, I was more like a negative five in terms of relaxing, and my mind started to finish his counting. Eleven, twelve, thirteen, and I couldn't seem to stop my mind from counting. Why in the world would he ask an OCD person to count?

Fifty-five, I have to stop counting...eighty-five, okay blank out the counting...ninety-one, I must stop counting....ninety-nine. Nighty-nine bottles of beer on the wall...okay, stop, seriously. You need to go back to the sexy man's voice and do what he's telling you to do.

I gave myself a couple more pops to the head, and I tuned in on his voice. He told me that I was now in that meditative mindset to find true peace. We were definitely not in the same place because I was still counting the beers on the wall.

I tried to focus, harder and harder I tried to focus! My legs were tucked into my body, and I was rocking back and forth. I had to get there. I was in a push-up position, and I tried so hard to get to that place. He told me to blank out my mind and to search for the face of true divinity. I was searching...searching! He said listen to what the voice of the Divine was telling me. I heard it! I heard it!

It said, "Hey, Ginny, did you order a pizza?"

Why did God sound like my roommate? I would think He would have a deeper voice, but that's cool that He likes pizza. The next thing I knew, there was a knock on my door, and my roommate barged in and turned on the light.

"Hey, pizza dude is here, and I don't have any money."

I stopped the video, took out my headphones, and tried to stand up. My body felt like it had just gone through a kickboxing class and not a meditation session. As my roommate and I were eating the pizza I must have ordered in between my pee or chiropractor appointment break, I went back online. This time I typed in "anxiety reducing therapy" and scrolled through the list of therapists in my town. It was probably best to leave the meditation to the professionals.

Goodbye, Michael Sealey. I felt like we had a good run, but we must break up now. I will miss your sexy voice and your handsome face, but it's best for both of us if we let each other go. And with that, I finally let go.

Chapter 2

De-stressing Techniques for the Wired

Since yoga and meditation didn't work out for me, I decided to try a massage. I feel like the only action a single person gets on a regular basis is getting a massage. My mom sent me a gift certificate for a massage along with a book titled *How to be Married in a Year.* Why does our society treat singlehood as a disease that must be cured? I immediately made an appointment for my massage because the message on the gift card said, "You really need to de-stress and calm your anxious mind. Enjoy!"

My booking phone call caused me a lot of undue stress. I had no idea there were so many options when it came to a massage. Swedish, deep tissue, combo, sports, reflexology, de-stress package, hot stone therapy, and that's just to name a few. After you pick your type of massage, you must decide the length of your session and if you want to fly solo or add a buddy. I ended up telling the receptionist that I just needed a rubdown, alone, and for the cheapest amount of time possible.

I'm sure she marked me as a shady client before my first visit.

When I arrived, I was pleased to find that my massage therapist was a female named Ruth. I mean, getting partially naked for either gender is extremely awkward, but at least I didn't have to worry about her giving my body a number. She went over the rules, disclaimers, and legal documents, and made me sign a bunch of papers. My signature was probably required because I was marked as a shady client, and then she told me to undress and get under the blanket face-up.

Before she left, she pointed to the sign on the wall: "Please leave your underwear on during the entire massage." What? Like what kind of place was this? Did people go commando when getting a massage? And the words "the entire massage" stuck out to me. Did people get going and then say, "Well these are a little too snug. Whoops! There they go!" I made sure my high-waisted granny panties were securely fastened before takeoff, and I began to wonder about my bra. A bra is considered underwear, so should it stay on for the entire massage?

I didn't want to break any of the rules since I had already been red-flagged. I decided to go for it, and I threw my extremely used, sweat-stained, sagged-out sports bra on the chair, and I got under the covers face-up. About five minutes later there was a knock on the door.

"Are you ready?"

"Yes, thanks for asking."

Ruth walked into the room and heaved an irritated sigh and said, "You're in the bed wrong."

"Huh, you said face-up, and I *am* face-up."

"Yeah, but your feet are in the headrest, and you basically undid the sheets to get like that. Was that not your first clue that your head was at the wrong end?"

"Well now that you point it out, yes, but when I get nervous, I can't think. Can you face the 'keep your stuff on the whole massage' sign while I rearrange myself?"

Ruth kindly turned around and focused her deep thoughts on the underwear warning banner while I got settled in correctly.

"Okay, I'm ready. Sorry about that."

Ruth had no response. In fact, she just dug in and started to go to town. I didn't think it was normal to scrunch up in pain and scowl during a massage. However, I had put my feet in the headrest, so by no means was I an expert on the subject. On a side note, at a gyno visit you put your feet in the cradle. I know this because I fear those jaws of life! I just assumed my feet went in the massage cradle too!

I found myself getting really anxious and definitely not "de-stressing" as I was ordered to do. In fact, my inner dialogue was going a hundred miles an hour:

Holy shit, this is really hurting. I wonder if I can say something...nope, better not, because next to the panty sign is a no talking sign. Can I tell her to lighten up? I wonder when she will turn me over...when she turns me over, I wonder if she will notice my cellulite, back fat, moles, freckles, and all of my wobbly parts... Ouch, what is that technique? Is she using her elbow now instead of her hands?

Wait, that's not her elbow. Is that her forearm? That's a strong forearm. What happened to the kneading technique? She isn't kneading bread, that's for sure. Wait, why is she slapping my arms, and slapping down my legs? Please make it stop... Now she's massaging my scalp...okay that's better... What? She's yanking my hair, and I need all of that to stay in place.

She's moving to my face...oh no, I told her I had sinus issues today. Okay, she's now pulling apart my face with so much force that I might as well be plastered up against a glass door, face first. I need to say something. I have to say something, but no talking, and no taking off underwear. Oh crap, are my panties still on? With all this excitement I'm not sure. They could have flown off. How much longer is this torture session going to last? I think I'm about to have a panic attack. Thank goodness I only signed up for a thirty-minute session!

Focus on your breathing! I can't breathe with my nostrils pulled apart. Oh, wait, actually I can breathe so much better than when I came in. Thanks, Baby Ruth! Oh my, now she's beating and pounding all over my whole body. Okay, now I have to say something before she fractures a rib.

"Okay, all done. You feel better now?"

"Um, what?" I replied in a voice that sounded like I had just been punched in the jugular. "Uh, sure, thanks."

"Get dressed and meet me out front in five minutes. Don't fall asleep."

Was that another rule and a posted sign that I missed?

I got up and tried to catch my breath and get my bearings. What just happened? And this was supposed to be pleasurable and de-stressing? Hell to the no!

I quickly dressed to stay within the five-minute rule and hurried to the front. Rue-Rue wasn't waiting for me at the front, only the receptionist, whom I had told on the phone that I wanted a rubdown. That was not my idea of a rubdown! She asked me if I wanted to pay with a credit card or cash. I slid her my gift card and she tapped her finger by the tip sign after she ran the card. I didn't think one typically added in a tip after they had been bullied, but I was too afraid to break another rule. I quickly reached into my purse and grabbed the only cash I had and prayed it was a decent enough amount to not embarrass myself.

Since my massage experience caused me a hefty bill at the chiropractor instead of de-stressing me, I decided to give hypnosis a try. I looked online, after my failed attempt at meditation and current massage flop, and I perused some articles on how hypnosis can help relieve stress and anxiety. It claimed to help you achieve internal peace and happiness...what everyone wants! This false promise was made to me by way of meditation and massage, but maybe hypnosis was the real deal! I figured it was time to give it a try because I am no quitter.

I crawled into my bed, turned out the lights, turned on the fan, plugged in my headphones, and scrolled through YouTube for the perfect video. I was still really confused as to the difference between hypnosis and meditation, but maybe hypnosis takes you deeper and it's more of a euphoric experience?

You know, like in the movies when you see a hypnotist turn someone into a duck, but after they have been brought back to reality with the snapping of fingers, they have no recollection of their run as a duck. That's some deep shit. I noticed that my man Michael Sealey did hypnosis too, but we'd had a bad break-up, so I decided to choose another person—I went with a female this time.

I chose the video that said, "Hypnosis for Relieving Anxiety and Deep Sleep." Good choice. I couldn't sleep too well these days either, so if a hypnotist could turn people into ducks and make them stop smoking, surely this method could put me to sleep. I pressed play. I was excited! Wait, I wasn't supposed to be excited; I must stay calm for it to work.

The voice began by telling me not to listen to this video while I was driving or operating heavy machinery. Well, I didn't plan on driving in my bed, but I wondered if my sleep apnea machine counted as heavy machinery or if any of the other toys under my bed fell in the above category. Then she told me to take deep breaths. Geez, again with the breathing; these people really liked you to focus on your lung capacity. I started to take deep breaths, and then she said all hypnosis was self-hypnosis, and at any time I could wake up from this video.

What...I can't hypnotize myself? That's why I'm listening to you, and if I can wake up from the video at any time, how is it supposed to put me to sleep? I started to think I'd picked the wrong video—maybe I should have gone back to my main squeeze. But I couldn't. I had come too far, and I had to keep going.

I closed my eyes and tried to focus on the sound of her voice, but my mind was saying, *This isn't working, this isn't working, you're still awake, you're still awake.* I tried to calm myself down, but every time she said, "You are getting sleepy," my mind said, *No I am not.* Then she was back to the breathing and talking about how I was going to get sleepy, but I was not sleepy.

I tried to focus on her words and the damn breathing, but I was breathing so hard that my throat began to hurt. I inhaled so much of the Vicks VapoRub, which I had on my feet to cure my foot fungus, that I began to lose feeling in my right nostril.

"You are getting sleepier and sleepier the deeper we go," she said in a very hypnotic voice. Then my mind said, *No I am not. I am still awake. I am still awake. This isn't working. I knew it wouldn't work. I can't be a duck.*

I tried to tell myself to calm down and relax. I was positive it had only been ten minutes, and it would probably take the whole video to get me to fall asleep and de-stress. Suddenly the video stopped. I looked down at my phone because I was sure that during my tossing, turning, and angry two-year-old tantrum moments, I must have paused it. It was over. That was why it stopped. It was over! I tried to tell myself that it was okay.

No one can fall asleep and relax, turn into a duck, or stop smoking in ten minutes. As I closed out the video, I happened to look at the time and realized the video was an hour and a half long! I guess I didn't do so well with my "self-hypnosis" session. My self sucked at hypnosis. Next time I would try it while driving or operating heavy machinery, and then I knew I could fall asleep!

Hypnosis isn't for the anxious. Can you imagine if I were to try to hypnotize someone? It would go something like this:

Okay, lie back and get comfortable. Try to relax and close your eyes. You need to know that all hypnosis is self-hypnosis, so you are really doing this to yourself, and you can wake up at any time. Well, you aren't really doing this to yourself, as I am your guide, so that's kind of a load of shit, but I have to say it, as it's one of the many disclaimers. Oh, and don't try to operate heavy machinery or drive while doing this. I don't think you would do this, as there isn't a way to drive a car in my office, and the only heavy thing in here is the couch. Don't try to lift the couch up while you're being hypnotized. Okay, does all this make sense?

Are you relaxed? Okay, I'm going to count to ten slowly, and after each number, you will feel more relaxed. One...two...three...four, five, six, oh, sorry I'll slow down...seven...eight, nine, ten. Are you there yet? Are you relaxed? Okay, now you are coming up to some water. You will slowly submerge into the water and feel so completely relaxed the deeper you go.

Here you go, down, down, okay, you are all the way underwater now, but don't worry, I won't let you drown. Are you feeling relaxed?

I'm supposed to take you through several other scenarios, but let's just cut to the chase. Look ahead of you and see the person you want to become. Okay, there she is. That's you. All your issues are fixed, and you are that peaceful person. Sound good? Okay, let's just go with that. Now I'm supposed to wake you up slowly, but I really need to go to the bathroom, so wake up, wake up! Okay, great, do you feel better now? Cool, well grab your stuff and hurry out because I need to go to the bathroom before my next session. You're cured now. There is no need to call me back. All is fixed, and I never have to see you again. Take care and have a nice life.

I would be a terrible hypnosis guide!

I guess I just need meds. Heavy, sedating, calming meds. However, in my world, when you go that route, you open a whole host of other issues.

"Yes, Dr. Lincoln, this one did work for my anxiety, but it causes endless constipation, and I am a regular girl."

"No, that one didn't work for my anxiety, and it says on the website that it can cause anxiety. Why would you give a person who has anxiety meds that can cause anxiety? You're saying that I'm making that statement because I'm anxious—well, maybe it's the meds you gave me that caused the elevated anxiety."

"No, that med didn't work because it caused me to have insomnia for two months."

"That one worked well for my anxiety, but it caused me to have so much anger I yelled at the kid at the coffee shop who burned my bagel. Following the incident, I had so much guilt, since I am a chronically nice person, that I cried for three days straight. I was also afraid I was going to be permanently banned from the coffee shop since I went back and apologized nine hundred times. Come to think of it, that med made my OCD worse."

"Speaking of crying, the second to last med you gave me caused me to cry for three straight weeks. Will that get better? If so, I can suck it up, butter cup."

"You think I need a new doctor because you are out of options for me? Are you quitting on me, doc? There is no I in team. If you are on my team, we DO NOT quit!"

"Good news, I finally found a med that works, except it causes me to have...well, I don't want to say this out loud since this is a virtual visit, and I'm afraid we are being recorded. Okay, I'll go for it...it causes my lady parts to dry up."

I am not a quitter. Today I became a quitter. I'll just move to California or Colorado and join a hippie commune and partake in their healing meds. I have no other choice in the matter. To quote my favorite rapper, Snoop Dogg, "If you got 'em, light 'em!"

Chapter 3

That One Time at Church Camp

The saying goes something like this: When God closes one door, He opens a window. However, in my life, when God closes a door, I beat it down, pick the lock, or crawl through the doggie door! I'm too busy focusing on the closed door to see the window open beside it!

I decided to open my eyes, get my head out of the clouds, and really start focusing on the signs that God was putting before me. I mean, true healing can only come from the Man Above, and God Himself knows I need some healing! God would agree that I live with my head up my ass and miss what's right in front of me.

Guess I shouldn't use the word ass when speaking on the topic of God—sorry about that. I'm working on that, along with the rest of my malfunctions. I am. My Gram used to tell me that to get closer to God, you must call Satan away. Like literally say out loud, "Satan, get behind me!" I tried this one time in the grocery store, but I didn't realize another shopper was slowly coming around the corner. He rolled up beside me with his cart and said, "My name isn't Satan, it's Bob."

Some days I wake up and I'm ready to put God first—which should be every day, I know. On these days I'm like, *God, please use me for Your purpose today, and let Your light shine through me unto others.* But on other days I wake up and my attitude is, *God, please don't use me today. Today I want to veg out, play on my phone, and watch reruns of* 90 Day Fiancé. This is horrible—I know.

Do you ever think that God gets tired of all our million prayer requests? Sometimes I picture Jesus being like, "Holy crap (and yes, my crap is holy), can you just handle your biz for one hour? One hour is all I'm asking. Like, Donna, I will bless the quilt you are making after this last episode. They're about to find out if the guy is getting catfished. I know he is, and who the real person behind the sting is, but to see it all go down and the looks on their faces makes it even better!"

Needless to say, I'm certainly an amateur when it comes to things of a spiritual nature, but I think it can be traced back to my beginning. Not Genesis, but Ginny's beginning.

My relationship with God and church didn't start off so well. Every kid growing up that attends church is introduced to vacation Bible school and church camp. They look forward to these events. I had a good time at VBS. I managed not to break too many things or get asked to leave. Therefore, my mom thought it was time for me to take the next step...church camp!

Mice, falling and rolling down a steep hill, lost and abandoned in the woods, and a chapped ass (oh sorry—rear) all come to mind when I think of "that one time at church camp." It was supposed to be the time of my life, or at least it was for most kids. You know your week isn't going to be ideal when you find out that your camp counselor is old enough to play bingo with your grandmother while the rest of the counselors are barely pushing twenty. She advised us to call her Binkie.

The week began with the counselors taking all the kids on a hike. Well, all the counselors but mine. Binkie told our troop that she was going to stay behind and clean up the bunks to get rid of the mice and their droppings. However, we all knew it was because she wanted to get in a couple more cigarettes, and she didn't want to carry her oxygen tank with her on the hike. No judgment here; we all loved Binkie.

As we started up the hill, I was already breathing heavily, and my back was aching. At this point, Binkie would have been lapping me, and I was having trouble keeping my balance (this balance thing has been a problem since my childhood). By the time we got to the top, I was too tired and beat down to enjoy the view. They told us to find a quiet spot to pray and soak up the beauty of nature. I was doing my best to focus and talk to God, but somehow, I managed to move a bit too close to the back side of the mountain. When I got up, I slipped and fell backward...and rolled, rolled, rolled, and rolled some more, down the hill! After my hiking disaster, I decided to stay at a lower altitude for the remainder of my nature walks.

Next came a game of hide-and-seek in the woods. I have no idea what part of this scenario seemed like a good idea, but all the counselors went with it since the head counselor organized the festivities. Melissa, the boss, gave us a quick rundown of the area and told us where to go, where not to go, and how to get back to our campsite. Needless to say, I got lost in the woods, and no matter what direction I turned, I couldn't find my way back. I had a lot of talks with God during this time, but they weren't peaceful, as I was fighting off panic attacks and crying spells. Finally, I sat down on a tree stump and begged God to send someone to find me, or if He Himself could guide me safely to camp, I would be forever grateful, as I didn't want to die this way. The next thing I knew I heard a commotion in the bushes, but there was no fire.

"God, is that you?"

"No, it's me, Binkie. Now carry my oxygen tank and I'll get you back to camp safely. You know, you aren't the brightest bulb on the Christmas tree."

"I know, Binkie, thanks for saving me."

"You owe me two packs of cigarettes out of your camp allowance money when we get back."

The food that was served at camp was a mixture of cardboard and cement. I had already used almost half of my food allowance on Binkie's cigarettes, so I had no choice but to eat what they served. By day three it was starting to move things around in my body. I had so many bathroom visits that I started to get what we call in my family "chapped ass syndrome." Oh sorry, chapped rear syndrome. I didn't pack any Desitin,

Preparation H, or Vaseline in my church camp survivor fanny pack, so I had to make that embarrassing phone call home.

"Hello?"

"Hey, bro, let me talk to Mom."

"Aren't you at church camp? You better not be calling collect. Mom and Dad will kill you and make you work all summer to pay for the call. That's what happened to me."

"No, you were making 1-900 calls to people you weren't supposed to talk to. Now get Mom, it's an emergency."

"Ginny, are you okay?"

"I'm fine, Mom. I just have a problem with my...well, my backside."

"Your backside? What do you mean? Did you fall and hurt yourself?"

"No, it isn't on the outside—it's on the inside."

"What do you mean it's on the inside? Can you speak up? I can't hear you."

"You know like when a baby gets a diaper rash, and, Mom, I can't talk too loudly since there's a line of kids behind me."

"Let me make some adjustments on my phone. Okay, I can hear you now."

"Basically, I have chapped rear syndrome. Can you send me some medicine?"

"Oh...well, just tell your counselor to take you to the store. It will cost too much for me to mail it."

"I don't want to ask her and have to tell her what it's for. Why is everyone laughing in the background?"

"I had to put you on speaker phone, and your dad, brothers, and the neighbors are over here watching the game and heard you."

I hung up the phone and had to do the walk of shame back to my cabin (a slow walk of shame with minimal friction to my cheeks, the cheeks not located on my face) and over to Binkie's bunk to talk to her.

"Binkie. Are you awake?"

"What the...? I am now. What do you want? It's like midnight. Go to bed."

"Binkie, it's only 8:15. Can you take me to the store?"

"What...what do you need at the store?"

"I would rather not say. Can you just take me?"

"Nope, I ain't getting out of bed at this hour unless you tell me what it's for."

"Well, you see, I, uh, I've been going to the bathroom a lot lately, and it's causing a problem with my, well, my backside."

"You mean you have chapped rear syndrome? Why didn't you just tell me? I've had that all week. Go over to my makeup bag and there's some medicine in there just for that."

"Thanks, Binkie, you're a lifesaver...again!"

"Well, that just cost you another pack of cigs out of your allowance!"

By the time my mom picked me up from church camp, I was in bad shape. I had never been more excited to see that beat-up, sky-blue minivan in my whole life. As we drove away, my friend started in on how exciting her week had been with all the friends she met, the incredible experiences she had, and the things she learned. I recapped my experience in my head: I fell down a hill, slept with mice, got lost in the woods, got a chapped rear, and church camp ended up costing me twenty-five dollars in cigarettes.

I can't say that I got closer to God or learned anything significant during my suffering, but then there was Binkie. Maybe God sent me Binkie because He knew I was going to have a rough go. No matter what you're going through, there is always a Binkie hiding in the shadows. Even if she smells of cigarettes, hates life, curses, carries an oxygen machine that squeaks, and constantly complains, she is still your Binkie!

I'm glad the Minion movies didn't come out back then! I look like their twin sister!

Chapter 4

Diet and Exercise—Hard Pass

I wore an orange tent-like muumuu dress to a funeral. I'm sure the person who passed away was looking down from heaven and telling God what an idiot I was for looking like a giant peach at his memorial service! My response, if I were granted access to speak directly to the above parties regarding the matter, would be, "Well, I am chunky, and I can't focus on style and appropriate dress, only covering 'it' up."

I would have chosen a more appropriate color, such as black, but the only sizes left in black were XS-S. Like people who wear those sizes need black! They could look slim in a horizontally striped print! I could have chosen the color plum instead of peach, but then I would closely resemble Barney, the unfortunately happy weirdo from years past.

Due to my funeral outfit, and the fact that I felt like crap, I decided it was time to get after it, turn my life around, and hit the gym. I'd purchased a gym membership, but since I couldn't find a close parking spot on several occasions, I stopped going. During my hiatus, I can't say I missed my workouts. My favorite part of my workout is when it's done and I'm leaving the gym, but then the realization I must come back and start over tomorrow hits me, and I get grouchy.

I have never been a big fan of the classes offered at the gym, and as previously stated, yoga and I don't get along. I tried step aerobics, but apparently, I sounded like I was entering a Stomp competition, and I was asked to leave and never return. My friend asked me to go with her to a class called "Zumba," where you shake your groove thang. I told her I only dance in the dark around people who have been drinking. She then tried to get me to go to a pole dancing class, and I denied her again. I told her I would only dance around poles if the room was so dark that I couldn't see my hand in front of me and dollar bills were being thrown in my direction.

I finally gave in and attended a class with her called "Body Pump," where you lift weights to the beat of music. My weights fell off my bar and hit the lady beside me in the head, and she was rushed to the hospital. Surprisingly, my friend never asked me to attend another class with her.

Since I was banned from most all the classes in the gym, I decided to start my own circuit weightlifting program. I got a hernia from putting a suitcase in my trunk, so my goal from the start was to build muscle mass. I began by using the lightest weights possible. This venture was deemed unsuccessful since I thought I tore my rotator cuff while doing a shoulder press.

I decided to ditch the weights and use the resistance band. That worked for a bit until my band came loose from the pole I had it tied to and popped me in the eye; I now have a detached retina.

My next exercise attempt came in the form of rock climbing. This doesn't work so great if you are deathly afraid of heights. I found this out halfway up Mount Everest and the seven-year-old beside me kindly helped me down to safety.

I gave up on the workout sessions and decided to focus solely on my eating. My cousin, who is a nutritionist, said when it comes to diet and exercise the ratio is 80/20, with 80% being the diet. Since I had drastically failed at the 20%, due to my failed exercise attempts, I put all my focus on dieting. She told me once I started eating healthy, the unhealthy food wouldn't taste good, and my body would crave nutritious foods. This is the biggest lie out there.

When I walk through the grocery store, my body yearns for Little Debbie cakes and nacho cheese Doritos on aisle nine. I must fight the urge to not pick up a pizza on the way home from work each day. The hardest part for me with the diet was giving up soda. Once again, the theory is if you stop drinking this blissful drug in the form of liquid, your body will find it to taste too sweet and will stop craving it. This is another gigantic lie! After two weeks of no soda, I allowed myself a sip of Pibb Xtra at the convenience store, and the clerk had to pull me off the machine because I was doing a keg stand. It tasted so good my sip turned into a pint.

Diet logging is so miserable. It's like keeping a record of your daily failures for your constant review. I would rather record my binge eating sessions on my cheat days. Those are of epic proportions, and I totally rock those cheat days. For example:

Breakfast: Two glazed donuts, Dr Pepper

Lunch: Fried chicken, fries, toast, Dr Pepper

Snack: Popcorn at movies, Milk Duds, Dr Pepper, and the rest of my niece's popcorn

Dinner: Pizza, lots of it, could possibly be a whole pizza, Dr Pepper

Snack in the middle of the night because I can't sleep: One piece of cake, followed by another, and then quite possibly the whole pan, even after I put water in the pan...I ate around the water

Water: Less than six ounces

Workout: Negative, Ghost Rider

Now that's some good eating! Besides, it shouldn't matter what I eat. I'm taking that Garcina Cambogia supplement Dr. Oz swears by, and all the celebrities take, and he says you can maintain normal eating habits. Well, I must have gotten a defective bottle because that shit ain't working.

I also hate the whole activity tracker craze—yet another reminder I failed that day. "Ginny, you have taken one hundred steps today. Great job, you loser." Plus, my workouts are so insignificant that I can't even track my steps doing my routine because I am not actually taking steps when I'm strolling on the stationary bike.

It would be great to have an activity tracker that gives you points for being lazy and not meeting your goals. Like, "Way to go, Ginny. You met your goal of doing absolutely nothing and clicking the remote all day! Your finger strength is amazing. I give you an extra hundred points for drinking less than four ounces of water...that takes talent!" I could really get on board with a plan like that!

With so many diets out there, it's hard to pick one and stick with it or to even know if the one you picked is the right one for you. Better yet, it's hard to know if you are even doing the one you picked correctly. I don't understand the difference between a paleo diet and a gluten-free diet. I thought all things paleo were gluten-free, but not all food items on a gluten-free diet are paleo. Or maybe it's the other way around? Upon this realization, I sat down and cried because I still couldn't understand the difference between the two—plus I wanted a donut.

I tried introducing superfoods such as kale, spinach, and kefir to my diet, but I don't know what kefir is. I like the actor Keifer Sutherland, and I would like to smoke some reefer, but I can't because it isn't gluten-free.

The worst of the worst diets is a yeast-free diet to get rid of a problem called candida overgrowth. I'm guessing this diet originated in Canada. My doctor wrote the instructions for this diet on a sheet of a paper, a list of supplements to be taken three times a day, along with drinking seventy-two ounces of water. What a beatdown!

If anyone asked me what I was up to while I was on this diet, I would respond with, "Well, I can't hold down a job because all I'm doing is trying to eat healthy, drink water, and manage my supplements. I must check my yes and no list before I eat anything, I pee every fifteen minutes, and I have to journal to keep up with the nine hundred supplements I'm supposed to take each day, three times a day."

On this particular diet, if you eat something on the no list, and a lot of it, you are basically set back to day one even if you were on day twenty. You can't eat any sauces, because sauces have sugar. Basically, if it tastes like cardboard, you can eat it. If it has any flavor or brings you any kind of joy in life, you can't eat it. Have you ever tried eating tuna without any salad dressing or mayo on it? It's like giving a dog peanut butter and watching him chew and then taking his water away. I was supposed to make it two weeks on this diet and then I could add fruit...oh yippee, fruit! I made it two days and then I punched a wall halfway through day three when I realized I couldn't have ketchup on my meat.

Through all of this, I realized that a healthy lifestyle just isn't in the cards for me. It isn't for the weak at heart, and apparently, I am weak at heart. I mean, my heart is probably super weak due to all the fried food, but I have accepted this. I have accepted I will never meet my fitness tracker goals each day, and I only use my tracker to check my text messages and phone calls. I have accepted that the ladies at the donut shop and Raising Cane's Chicken know my name, and I consider them to be my close friends. I have accepted that I would rather lie in my bed watching Netflix than go out to a social gathering where I must wear pants that don't have an elastic waistband.

I have accepted that if I drink water all day, I live in the bathroom. If I drink soda, I can go for hours on end without having to pee. I have accepted not drinking seventy-two ounces of water a day; I will just go over to my buddy John's house every morning and get an IV of fluids (he's a paramedic). This way I can drink Dr Pepper all day. Life is about acceptance, and I will gladly accept the venti, extra whip, whole milk latte (yes, I am drinking milk, and it is cow's milk) over the green tea any day! Now if you will excuse me, I just had a sip of water, and I'm headed to the bathroom.

Chapter 5

God or Tacos?

S ometimes God puts things in your heart to say and share with others. Sometimes it isn't God at all; it's indigestion from the street tacos you ate. I really have trouble deciphering between the two, but this felt more like God, not tacos! Oh, how I love both...but tacos aren't allowed on my stupid-ass healthy diet. God, I'm sorry I said a bad word! I'm working on it!

I'm nervous. I'm just going to put it out there. It's hard to be an entertainer of any sort in today's world with so many people finding fault in your work and looking for things that might not be there. As I stated before, I suffer from chronic "way too nice syndrome."

My family and friends laugh at me all the time—apparently, I am one big disclaimer! My comedy is meant to bring joy to others, and not offend, but sometimes people take offense. I'm an OCD, overly nice, worried-about-what-people-think comedian who has a fear of upsetting people. We all have our issues! Please know that everything I try to do comes from a good place. I think many comedians carry this burden.

The following chapter, "We Have a Runner," was written about twelve years ago and has since been edited and tweaked. It is mostly about situations in which I panic, like all the time, but there is story about a lockdown drill we had when I was teaching high school. This disclaimer is for that portion of the chapter.

I don't even know how to say what I am trying to say here. This is just straight from my heart, and please forgive me if this isn't said how it should be said. I am truly struggling with this.

My heart breaks for those who have lost loved ones in mass shootings. I can't even begin to fathom what you go through every day and each time there is another shooting. I don't know what to say to parents who have lost their children in these horrific events. All I can do is pray for you and for our country. Please know you are all in my thoughts and prayers, and I am so, so sorry.

By no means am I trying to make light of these horrific events by discussing a lockdown drill in a humorous way. What I am trying to portray is how big of a malfunction and panicker I am when it comes to difficult moments—moments when you need to be strong. I just choke.

The humor is in trying to do it right because I do take it seriously, and then I fail by trying so hard. I'm also attempting to show you what these situations can be like from a teacher's perspective. By no means am I representing all teachers here, just me, but I will be the first to tell you that during that drill (which we thought was real) I was scared.

I think many teachers feel this way. I was scared every day in my classroom that I wouldn't be able to protect my students due to my own failure and ability to remain strong, as well as the situations in which teachers are put in each day. I felt like a policeman without weapons when I went to work. I can tell you we are doing the best we can to protect our kiddos, but we feel scared and ill-equipped each day.

Thank you to all the teachers and staff who put their lives on the line each day for our kiddos. You are appreciated beyond words. I hope this chapter can make you smile from the standpoint of what we deal with daily and how we try our best yet always feel we come up short. A special shout-out to all the kiddos out there attending school. You shouldn't have to go into a learning and enriching environment with fear. You are the heroes too!

I know I won't win with this disclaimer and chapter because many may find fault in what I tried to do here, but please know my intentions are good. I just wanted you to see what it's like for teachers who truly care but make mistakes.

I must go now. All this talk of tacos has made me hungry. Plus, discussing some of the above controversial topics has made my "overthinking and worrying" stomach upset. So I'm off to Taco Bell to soothe my worries with tacos. A message for my holistic doctor and trainer...you can suck it, sometimes a girl just needs some tacos! But I love ya!

With love,

Ginny ♥

Chapter 6

We Have a Runner

MMA fighter Ronda Rousey is legit. I sometimes imagine that I am her, and when I walk into a room, people shake in fear and get up to give me their seat. The sad thing is if you were to put me in the ring with her when the bell rang, I would scream (the highest pitched scream you have ever heard), throw my gloves at her, and run out of the ring. In my mind, I would love to be like Wonder Woman or Black Widow in terms of looks and ass-kicking abilities, but I'm more like Nacho Libre!

Yes, when it comes down to it, I run. I run when there's no place to run. When I'm in a tight spot or if something is about to go down, there is no fight in me, but my flight is at full speed. My flight isn't even that productive. It's more like a dog running in place or trying to run when he's on a leash and he gets clotheslined and brought back to the starting point. I was once stuck in an elevator because I forgot to push the floor button. The elevator stopped, the lights went off, and I began to run laps inside the elevator. An hour later the lights came on, and the elevator headed to the lobby floor. My elbow must have hit the L button during one of my lap sessions, as my brain never thought to pause and push the button!

I'm such a panicker in stressful situations that I even panic when I know it's coming. When I was teaching high school, we were told ahead of time we would have fire drills, and we were even given the exact time. However, when the fire alarm would go off, I would scream and put my hands over my head. The kids would walk around me to safety. The worst of all school drills was the lockdown.

One morning, I arrived fairly early, and I was heading to my classroom, but I stopped to say hello to a teacher down the hall from me. All of a sudden, we heard a recording come over the speaker system: "We are in a high-level lockdown. Please follow protocol."

The recording was playing over and over, and it wasn't our principal's voice. It was a pre-recorded voice. My first thought was that our principal was in hiding, or had been hijacked, and this was the real deal. The worst part was when I looked up at my friend, who was older than I and a calm veteran teacher, I saw panic in her eyes.

This was it. It was go time. My friend gathered her stuff and the kids around her, and she headed to her closet to lock everyone in. I, on the other hand, took off on my laps. I was so out of it that I didn't even hear my friend calling my name and trying to stop me. I headed out of her room, and I was so focused on getting to my room that I chop blocked another teacher coming into the building.

Tim Riggins would be proud of my effort. I had no recollection of this, and I still don't. I only know it happened because I was told afterward that I owed her two teas from Taco Bell. Apparently, neither she nor her tea survived my chop-block. It must have been a Ronda Rousey-like-chop-block! As I headed down the hall, I was mindful to zigzag as I ran, and I gathered students along the way.

"Move...go, go, go...we have to get in my classroom behind the locked door."

I was supposed to remain cool, calm, and collected and be an example to the kids so that they wouldn't panic. Well, we were way past that! I continued to gather kids around me and get them into my room. My hands were shaking so badly that I dropped my keys twice as I tried to unlock the door. One kid strolled down the hall carrying a box of glazed donuts. He was not complying with my demands.

"Come on, let's go, get in my classroom." (But this was shouted as though I had been sucking on a helium balloon. The more I panic, the higher my voice gets!)

"What? What's going on? I don't want to come into your room."

"OMG, get in here! It's a high-level lockdown, this is not a drill. I repeat, THIS IS NOT A DRILL!"

At this point, he could tell I was serious and panicking because apparently, my voice had gone into screech mode. This scared him so badly that he threw up the box of donuts and they spilled all over the hall. Instead of leaving them behind, he decided it would be a good idea to start picking them up, all twelve of them.

"Leave the donuts. Your life depends on it!"

He ran toward my door and dove into my room. I realize now that was not the best thing to say to a kid in that situation, but it was go time and he wasn't listening. Drastic measures had to be taken. I made one last glance down the hall and saw no kids, but our history teacher was strolling down the hall with his pants sagging and headphones on while carrying his scantrons. He was the real OG.

"Mr. Easton, get in here now!"

"What did you say? I had my headphones on jamming out to Tom Petty."

"I said get in my room now. We're in a high-level lockdown and it's go time!"

Mr. Easton was a true badass. He put his headphones back on, cranked up the tunes, and strolled into my room.

Meanwhile, the kids in my room began to get restless and started asking a ton of questions. I looked down to find my cell phone and realized I'd left it in my friend's room; therefore, I couldn't contact anyone to find out what was going on because the classroom phones were down.

"Miss, are we going to have to sit in here all morning with the lights off and the filing cabinet and desks shoved against the door? Also, can you put the bat down and stop pacing? You're making us nervous. Are you going to buy me a dozen donuts since you ruined mine?"

It was really hard for me to focus on what he was saying, as I was trying to resist the urge to do my laps around the room. I had donut boy staring me down for causing him to lose his donuts, Mr. Easton seemed to be put out with me, and the rest of the kids were posting stuff on social media and taking selfies as though nothing was happening.

Finally, after fifteen painful minutes, we got the clearance that everything was all good. "Teachers, please pardon the confusion. Our alarm system went off and that causes the recording to go off over and over."

The kids got up and raced to the door. "Well, it will take us an hour to get out of here because we have to take down all of the barriers to the fort she made!"

Donut boy was pissing me off. Did he know all the sacrifices I had made for him in the last ten minutes? The kids and Mr. Easton finally exited my room, and I found myself enraged. You mean to tell me all of that was due to a malfunction with the alarm system? Are you kidding me? I was so stressed out by the series of events that had transpired and finding out it was a faulty alarm that I walked out into the hall and grabbed one of the donuts off the floor and ate it.

Later that day I discovered the tea spillage caused a lot of stress. Apparently, the teacher in the room by the spill was locked in her closet with Dave, who suffers from extreme OCD and asks thirty questions per minute. We could totally be best friends under different circumstances. Dave could see the tea running down the hall from his peephole in the closet (that sounds kind of bad), and he had a giant panic attack because he thought it was blood.

My next epic failure came when we had a huge fight down the hall from my room. I heard the screams and commotion and proceeded to run down the hall to see what was going on. Two girls were going at each other...Ronda Rousey-style, but with hair extensions and false fingernails flying everywhere! My neighbor teacher stepped in to break up the fight, and another teacher came running down.

"Ginny, don't just stand there watching, go get help. I'm getting my butt kicked here!"

I tend to be a lot like the character Walter Mitty in the movie *The Secret Life of Walter Mitty* during stressful situations. I zone out and daydream of something epic I would do. I was envisioning grabbing both girls and holding them against the wall at the same time, one in each hand, and saying in a deep, authoritative voice, "Ladies, we've got to calm down. We must love each other and treat each other with respect. Besides, you are ruining your awesome hair and nails, and they looked good!" Then I would set them down gently because I had them held way up the wall, and they would apologize to me, each other, take a selfie like they are besties again, and then walk away.

"Ginny, for the love of all that is holy and just in this world, go get help. NOW!"

"Oh, sorry, okay, I'm on it!"

Instead of turning around and walking two feet down the hall to get the two teachers who taught law enforcement and were former cops, I ran two halls over, and screamed at the top of my lungs, "Help, we need some help out here!"

The pre-calculus teacher, who was seventy-five, came out in her rolling chair.

"I'm here. What can I do to help?"

"Oh, sorry, Ms. Garon, but we need help in a bigger size."

Finally, after screaming down three hallways, I found Mr. Vernon, who was about 6'4" and 300 pounds. We ran down the halls (well I use the term "run" loosely, as I have a bum knee and Mr. Vernon didn't move too quickly, but we did the best we could). By the time we got to the fight, everyone had cleared out.

"Hey, thanks for getting help an hour later, Ginny!"

"Man, I'm sorry. I thought I was doing good to get Mr. Vernon. I just knew he could break up the fight. I mean, he's a big boy!"

Mr. Vernon, who was now hunched over and wheezing from our quick jog, glared at me over his glasses.

"Well after you left, one of the kids just walked two feet down the hall and got the two law enforcement teachers to help me. What were you thinking?"

I was thinking to myself that I did great because I didn't take off on my usual ten-mile relay race, but apparently it wasn't enough. From then on, I was labeled the "panicker," and other teachers would run up behind me and yell "fight" just to see if I would start my laps.

These teachers didn't know my history. They didn't know that two years ago while at the lake with friends,

I bailed from my jet ski in the middle of the lake because it was getting too close to the boat. My boyfriend at the time had to jump in the lake and swim after the jet ski. When I can't run, I jump ship (or jet ski) and that's my version of running. The amazing comedian Whitney Cummings in her show *Whitney* defends why she ran when she and her boyfriend were being mugged by saying, "That's what you're supposed to do. Everyone knows when a couple gets mugged you are supposed to run in opposite directions. He can't shoot both of you!"

I agree with her completely, and my body does this naturally. If my boyfriend and I were to get mugged, I too would run and scream at the mugger, "Get him! He has more money in his wallet and his credit cards aren't maxed out."

I'm like Lloyd in the movie *Dumb and Dumber* when Harry throws the saltshaker over his right shoulder and hits Sea Bass in the head. Lloyd, with his head down, points his finger at Harry to make sure he gets the blame. I would shove my friend under the bus any day to save my own skin. I would do all these things in the above situations without even knowing I was doing it.

So given my past, I was pleased with myself for not running laps during the fight and actually going and getting help. The fact that the help came ten minutes after the fight was over is irrelevant to me. I'm choosing to focus on the positive, and I'm so proud of my baby step improvements. However, it's time to face the cold hard facts: If you're in a tight spot and need a Ronda Rousey-type, I am not your girl. But I make an awesome Forrest Gump. "Run, Ginny! Run!"

Chapter 7
Worldly Travels on a Yellow Dog

I have always been fascinated with windows. This fascination began as a young child and has continued into adulthood. When I was younger, I would find myself looking out my bedroom window and contemplating life, or contemplating it to the best of my abilities, seeing as how I wasn't the brightest of kids.

I remember looking out my window in my small room, filled with white wicker furniture and a host of creepy clowns, and seeing my older brother sneaking out in the middle of the night and speeding away in his girlfriend's Dodge Dart. I watched a number of basketball pickup games that always ended up being shirts versus skins (there were several boys that needed to be permanent members of the shirt team), and I saw many domestic showdowns with my "Git R Done" neighbors.

When I was in junior high, my family moved into a rent house that could have easily been on any horror flick. I ended up with the bedroom that had the attic. It wasn't like our previous house, where the attic was in the garage, and you gained access to it by pulling the string attached to the cut-out square in the middle of the ceiling.

After you pulled the string down, a set of old, creaking, wooden stairs came down and then your father, who was too heavy to use the stairs, would crawl up to get more "crap" that your mom had stored up there. Access to this particular attic in my new room was reached by going through the tiny door located in the middle of the wall. It looked like a door in a dollhouse, as not many people could fit through this tiny space.

My mom, whose stuff couldn't all fit in our four-bedroom house and storage room, made me store her white rocking chair in my room, in front of the attic door, since we were out of space. I have witnessed this scene play out in so many horror movies. You see a creepy figure rocking in the chair holding something you don't need to see, and then someone comes out of the attic and attacks you. I would replay this scene over and over each night in the dark while staring at the empty rocking chair that was in front of the tiny door, anxiously waiting for the door to open. Many, many sleepless nights in this room!

The best feature of this house was that the front door had a small window about halfway up located near the doorbell. I would go outside and ring the doorbell and watch my Jack Russell jump up and down and see his head pop up into the window over and over again. I am afraid my doorbell ringing escapades caused him to develop hip dysplasia and arthritis. I'm sorry, little buddy.

The following year we moved into a shiny new house, and my bedroom had a huge window with a window seat. My parents gave me the best room to make up for the therapy sessions I had to attend to recover from the scary movie that played out in my room every night in the rent house. Tiny doors and rocking chairs are hard things to get over. This window had a view of our seventy-five-year-old neighbor who would go out every morning, afternoon, and evening and smoke his cigar—shirtless and in his see-through boxers. This proved to be detrimental to my health, so I began to close the blinds and refrain from watching the world out of that window.

College brought about many windows to view the world from; in fact, I had a new worldview every year. I moved a total of seven times while in college, and all my bedrooms had windows. The view out of one window allowed me to witness the neighborhood cat, who was a male slut, mate with every female cat within a fifty-mile radius. I would always shut my blinds when this event was happening.

I saw a lot of naked people, some good, some really bad. I saw my neighbor, who was really drunk at the time, run up and down the street with nothing on but a trucker's ball cap. This wasn't anything out of the ordinary; this was college, people! I witnessed my roommate have a dozen fights with her boyfriend in the front yard, and every dog in the neighborhood used our front yard as a dumping ground.

After college, I moved to California, and I lived in an efficiency apartment, or that's what the ad in the paper said it was. It was more like a miniature single room, but it had an excellent window. I watched my neighbor toke it up every night via a joint, bong, or some other contraption that I never figured out. My other neighbor was an aspiring actress, and she chose to use the small space outside of my apartment as her practice stage. I sure hope she found another career because my ten-year-old niece performed better in her *School of Rock* play at the local church.

There was a homeless guy who frequently slept outside of my window. I would give him food and warm clothing, and every now and then he would smile at me, but most of the time he would flip me off. There was a fast-food restaurant fifty feet from my doorstep; it was responsible for the fact that I couldn't wear any of my clothes six months after I moved in. I got to see just how healthy that food really is—trust me, there are some things in life you don't need to see.

The most insightful windows of my life have been the windows of a school bus, aka yellow dog. I have taken many trips in this wonderful, luxurious vehicle, and I gained a great deal of knowledge from my sightings. For example, when I was in junior high, I looked out the windows of the bus as I put a stink bomb on the floor and stepped on it per a double dog dare by my friends. I learned that if you got caught, your coach would make you run until you threw up and your dad would beat your ass when you got home.

When I was in high school, my friends dared me, again, to moon the car behind us on a trip home from a basketball game. I put my small backside (man, I sure wish it was still that small and perky) up to the big window on the back of the bus and received several honks from the car trailing us. Little did I know that the driver of this car was our high school principal, and I was sent to the alternative campus for a brief stint following the mooning. To this day, I still don't know how she knew it was my backside in the window. This fact is still a little perplexing to me.

I became a high school coach for a brief time in my adult life, and I found myself taking many a trip on the big cheese. However, this time it was different. I had to make sure there wasn't a kid dropping stink bombs and mooning people if I wanted to keep my job. We would travel to exotic places like Dumas, Texas. The scenery of the small towns in West Texas is quite similar to the setting in a western movie. The terrain is full of bare, lifeless, dead ground and tons of blowing dirt.

A sandstorm, which is a rare event in many places of the world, is a reoccurring, once-a-week event for towns in West Texas. However, the people in these small towns are amazing, and that more than makes up for the lack of scenery. When I thought the sandstorm had passed, I would open the windows to get some fresh air. After athletic competitions, the bus smelled like my feet when I take off my tennis shoes after a long day. Instead of getting rejuvenated by the fresh air, I would find my face covered in dirt as well as an additional layer of grit around my mouth that was sticking to the lip gloss I just applied.

I witnessed memorable things through those windows on some of our adventurous travels. One time, we were traveling through a beautiful neighborhood, lost as usual because our bus driver couldn't find his way out of a parking garage, and I noticed a group of small children playing in a driveway. One boy, in particular, stood out because he had fire-engine-red hair and he was staring at our bus. I smiled and waved at him, but he flipped me off while chasing after the bus.

I had great philosophical talks with our bus driver, Vince, who hated kids. He spent most of his time watching the kids in his rearview mirror and yelling at them when they rose up to adjust their position so the springs in the seats would stop piercing them in the back. He reminded me of Chris Farley's character in the movie *Billy Madison* when he was driving the bus and constantly screaming, "No yelling on the bus!" He then proceeded to curse at the kids under his breath. This was Vince for sure. Vince got his license suspended when he hit a pole while filling up with gas at the local gas station, so we got a brief break from his tyranny for a couple of trips.

They say that our eyes are the windows of the soul, but I beg to differ. Actual windows give us more insight into our souls. I have learned so much in my life, and about myself, by looking through windows. For example, as a child, I learned that during a domestic dispute, it is best not to bring up your significant other's drinking and ball-scratching bad habits.

In my teenage years, I was taught that if you look at a seventy-five-year-old man naked, it will burn your eyes and your soul. In college, I discovered that some animals have weird mating habits and that college dudes who are in good shape look good when streaking. In California, I learned there is more than one way to smoke weed, and it isn't all in the form of a rolled joint. While coaching, I learned that not all redheaded little kids are cute and innocent, especially when they shoot you the bird, and not all bus drivers like their jobs, or kids. I never would have learned so many extraordinary life lessons if I hadn't taken a moment to look out the window.

Chapter 8

Bengay in the Night

I t began with a knee surgery...followed by another surgery, and then a bout of shin splints in the good leg. I guess it got tired of supporting the bad leg for so long, it finally had enough and gave out too. I was in so much chronic pain that I was having trouble sleeping. I felt like my sleepless nights were due to my chronic pain; however, it could be that the waistband of my pajama bottoms had gotten so tight it was cutting off my circulation.

My friend, who is a pharmacist, suggested I try some anti-inflammatory cream on all my aches and pains. I took her advice and perused the different types at the local CVS. I finally decided on a small tube of Bengay. I would like to think it was because I weighed the pros and cons of the ingredients and found it to be the best. However, it was more because I'm a tightwad, and that brand was on sale. Plus, I had a coupon! As I hobbled my way back to the car, I had a new glow; I just knew this was going to cure all my problems and help me get some much-needed rest.

I immediately took a hot shower when I got home and started the process of getting ready for bed. After the face washing, anti-aging eye/face/neck/chest creams, brushing, rinsing, flossing, night guard, teeth bleaching, eyelash/brow treatment, tweezing, plucking, and lastly, securing the breathing strip, I was ready to crawl in bed and slather on the new product.

Getting ready for bed is indeed a process the older you get. In my younger years, I would brush my teeth, take the towel used to dry my mouth, and wipe it all over my face and call it good.

As I took the lid off the Bengay and removed the plastic sticker covering the opening, my sinuses were immediately cleared by the potent, vapor-like smell, and my eyes began to water. I figured that it had to smell bad with all of the healing ingredients, but as long as it worked, I didn't care if I smelled like the old folks' home.

I began by rubbing it on my bum knee, then my shin, and then I decided to doctor the good leg and shin. I remembered my neck and jaw hurt, so I slathered on a thick amount there too. By the end of my ten-minute treatment, I had pretty much covered my whole body with half of the tube.

It started as an innocent scratch, but then it became deadly. After I had finished my bath of Bengay, my eyes began to itch and burn due to the smell. I made the mistake of scratching my eye with my finger—the finger that was slathered in the product! Immediately my eye began to burn as though I had been stung by a bee directly in the eyeball!

I jumped up and threw the covers to the floor. This was not a good move, as my Chihuahua, Charlie, was flung across the room. He was a Bengay innocent bystander who was snuggled comfortably in the covers before they were thrown to the floor. I ran over and tried to console and comfort him. I checked him over as thoroughly as I could while using one eye.

He's going to need some Bengay in the morning when his injuries from being punted across the room settle in!

It was then that I realized I was petting him with the hand that had been slathered in the product and he was starting to scratch himself all over. I told Charlie he would have to "suck it up, buttercup" while I tended to my eye.

It was quite difficult reading the label of where not to put this product and what to do if this product got in the where-not-to-put-it parts when I was squinting and keeping my stinging eye shut. It basically said if you get the product in your eye, you must flush it out thoroughly and completely. I didn't want to have to open my eye, let alone drown it with water, but one must do what they have to do in tough times.

I tried to open my eye wide enough to give it a bath, but as soon as the air reached it, I kept closing it because the stinging was intense. I gave myself a couple of pep talks and opened my eye and gave it a shot of water. I did this about three times, and then I decided to take a break to check on Charlie.

Charlie had been scratching and licking for the last five minutes, and now he was doing the booty scoot across my bedroom rug. Perhaps that could be due to the Bengay or another issue, but at least he was moving, at quite a fast pace as a matter of fact, and this led me to believe that he survived the cover punt.

I went back to the sink and gave my eye two more shots of water and myself one shot of tequila to help the burning. When I was satisfied with my eye wash, I grabbed a baby wipe and went over to Charlie to give him a bath. Five minutes later, Charlie, who was smelling like a baby after a bubble bath, decided he was done with me and fled the scene.

I headed back to bed with my eye now stinging from the product and water burn, grabbed the discarded covers off the floor, and plopped down for some rest. Through all this commotion, I remembered I forgot to put Vaseline on my lips, something I do every night before going to bed, so I reached for the tub. I dug my finger into the jar and slathered it on my lips. Meanwhile, I guess Charlie had forgiven me, as he had managed to plop back up on the bed and settle into the covers.

Well, I used the wrong finger! I used the finger that I had used to slather on the Bengay, and during all my eye flooding, I forgot to wash my right hand! Immediately my lips were on fire. I was still experiencing the stinging from my half-opened eye and now my lips. I flung the covers off again, and Charlie went sailing to the floor for a second time! I felt so bad, but my lips felt like a Botox session gone significantly south, and I couldn't check on Charlie at the moment.

I grabbed the tube of Bengay and went back to the section on what to do when it got in the wrong parts. I assumed I was supposed to just wash it off, as with my eye, but now it said if it got in your mouth and you swallowed it, you must call this other number!

Oh crap, did it get in my mouth? Did I swallow it? What should I do?

Luckily, I remembered this time to wash my right hand before I started to wash my lips. I basically began to eat the bar of soap to make sure I completely and thoroughly washed out my mouth and lips. The stinging from my lips began to subside, but in my panic, I guess I started to cry, and every time I shed a tear it made my eye burn worse!

When would Bengay's attack stop?

I walked over to Charlie, who was now in the corner in a ball shaking from his second onside kick of the night, and I grabbed him up and apologized. We crawled back into bed, and I decided to not apply more product, of any kind, on any body part, for the rest of the night.

At 9:00 that morning, my cell phone rang and woke me up. It was my neighbor asking if she could come over and borrow some creamer. Apparently, during my Bengay raid in the night, I must have handled my phone, several items on my nightstand, my pillowcase, sheets, and bedspread, as the entire bedroom smelled of a night of...Bengay. When I answered the door, my neighbor met me with a look of horror on her face.

"Dang, how many drinks did you have last night, neighbor, and who gave you the shiner and a fat lip? I want all the juicy details!"

"You wouldn't believe me if I told you!"

My entire body hurt, from eyeball to toe, not to mention the fact that I looked like I spent the night in a bar (without any fun). When Charlie came around the corner to greet my neighbor, he was moving at a slow pace with a bit of a gangster limp. She gasped and screamed, "What the heck happened to you last night, and who let you take a dog into a bar? It looks like Charlie had a rough night too!"

Charlie and I both shot my neighbor a look and he wobbled to the couch.

"You need a beer, two Advil, some ice, a massage, and perhaps some Bengay. By the way, you're limping. Charlie too. Do they make Bengay for dogs?"

As soon as my neighbor said the B word, Charlie hid under the couch.

After adding creamer to my coffee, I tossed it at my neighbor, pointed her toward the direction of the door, and passed out on the couch with Charlie shaking underneath it.

Chapter 9

Andrews and Acupuncture

C harlie and I were extremely sore after our battle with Bengay. He told me he was throwing in the towel and was probably just going to overdose on his Dasuquin, but I wasn't ready to give up on treatment options for my chronic aches and pains just quite yet. I am no quitter.

I had a friend who told me about the amazing healing components of acupuncture. She went on and on about how it basically cured her arthritis and headaches. I decided to give it a try. I was pleasantly surprised when I was able to get an appointment for the next day.

I arrived early for my appointment because I figured I would have to fill out a ton of paperwork, being a new patient. The receptionist greeted me with a friendly smile and handed me a single sheet of paper. She had pink hair and a nose ring, and her arms and neck were covered with tattoos. What a cool chick! She apparently wasn't a sissy like me and afraid of needles. She told me that since this procedure wasn't covered by insurance, very little paperwork was required. I had no argument with this, so I relaxed the rest of the time and looked through some of the magazines on the table beside me.

The lobby had a bohemian feel to it, and there were several candles burning around me and by the receptionist's desk. After about ten minutes I was getting a headache from the smell of the candles, and I was starting to get nervous about the idea of having tons of needles stuck in my body. In fact, the realization of what I was about to do sank in, and I was having second thoughts.

How in the world does poking someone with needles help cure chronic pain? Sounds like that's going to add more pain and make the current pain worse because you aggravated it with needles!

My stream of thoughts continued as the technician came out and called my name.

"Hello, Guinea. My name is Gavin, how are you?"

"Hello, Gavin, I'm good, but my name is pronounced as 'Gin-ny.'"

"Oh, right, right, my bad. I'm sorry about that."

"No worries, it happens all the time."

I was taken aback at first glance because Gavin was in his mid-twenties and had spiked-up hair, a half-buttoned collared shirt, skinny jeans, and Vans. He looked like he was about to go to the skate park instead of performing a medical treatment. I was expecting an older gentleman and perhaps someone that looked like Gandhi or Morgan Freeman—someone that wisdom oozed out of. He advised me to lie down on the table, and he briefly went over the ins and outs of acupuncture.

He talked about the "Yin and Yang Theory" and something about my "qi" (pronounced chi). The only thing I could think about was the Chia Pet I'd had in eighth grade, and I wasn't sure what that had to do with acupuncture. I guess it was related because when the needles were all over my body, I would look like a fully-grown Chia Pet!

"I noticed on your sheet that you shaded in several areas on your body where you have pain."

"Yes, I'm sure my sheet looks like a first grader used it as a coloring book, but it was hard to narrow it down to just one area."

"Well, we'll need to focus on just one treatment for today, so which hurts you the most?"

"I guess let's start with my jaw. I have nerve damage to the inferior alveolar nerve, the nerve they numb for dental procedures, and it makes it feel like I have a fifty-pound brick in the left side of my mouth. I'm also experiencing hypersensitivity, so the slightest touch sets it off."

"Bummer, that stinks. I'm really sorry."

"No worries. So many people have it so much worse, but I'm hoping acupuncture can calm down the nerve. Although, I am a little worried about poking needles in a place that's already super sensitive."

"Yeah, I can see why you might be worried."

I was hoping his response would be a bit more comforting and that maybe he might say he would position the needles in a way that it wouldn't hurt in that area. He didn't.

As he was rubbing down the spots with alcohol, he tried to explain the basic benefits of acupuncture. However, I was too focused on the needles about to go into my face and body to absorb what he was saying.

I wonder if a person who is about to shoot up on a drug of their choice gets this nervous before a needle poke? Why is it called recreational drug use? Recreation implies something fun, and there's nothing fun about needles!

As I looked around the room, it looked like something out of a horror flick. I was lying on a table in a dark room with candles burning around me. There was a small table beside me with needles, alcohol, and cotton swabs, and I was about to be poked and prodded by a guy who looked like Adam Levine.

This wasn't a bad thing by any means, as Adam is a hottie. However, at any moment while he was poking needles in me, I imagined that he might start singing the chorus to "Girls Like You." That might actually be nice, as long as the Adam Levine lookalike knew what he was doing because the torture session was moments away from starting!

"I changed my mind," he announced. "Since you have so many areas of pain, I think we'll just place needles all over your body and not just your jaw. I think this will help your overall pain. Does this sound okay?"

Before I could answer, he began by placing a needle in my foot.

"Ouch! What the heck? Why my foot? My feet don't hurt! They weren't shaded on the handout. Please refer to the handout!"

"Needles on your feet, toes, parts of your leg, forearm, and hands are standard to any treatment. I'm afraid if your whole body is 'on fire,' as you describe it, this may be a painful process. Should I keep going?"

I never back down from a challenge, of any kind, no matter how painful it is. I am not a quitter!

"Yes, just keep going. I can take it. It might be best to just stop at the end when it's done, rather than stop after each needle. Just rip the band-aid off quickly!"

He began with my toes and worked his way up from there. It felt like electric shocks all over my body, and he seemed to be using his entire stock of needles and then some. At one point my catlike reflexes kicked in when he was around my knee, and I might have kicked my leg up and knocked him in the face. I can't say for sure because the shocks were making it difficult to focus on anything other than when the next shock would come.

"Ginny, I think I'll have to stop telling you which body part I'm moving to next because you keep moving your body before I stick the needle, and I have stuck several soundly in the table underneath you."

"Sorry about that. I guess I'm subconsciously moving my leg when I know you're about to stab it. It's an involuntary reflex survival mechanism that I can't seem to stop. So yes, it's better for you to just poke the body part without telling me where the pain is coming from next."

We finally finished my entire body, and now it was time to move to my jaw. This I wasn't sure I could handle, as the left side of my jaw already felt like needles were poking it sans needles poking it.

"Okay, this part is going to hurt since you have nerve damage in this area. Do you want me to stop and we do that on another day?"

I leaned up and looked over my entire body to see millions of needles that he had strategically placed over almost every inch of my toes, feet, legs, arms, and hands. I then shot him a look that said it all.

"Okay, I see your point. We've come this far. Why stop now? Let me know if this gets too much to handle."

I would have given him the thumbs-up, but my thumb was basically stapled to my hand due to the ten thousand needles around it, so I gave him a "we-are-a-go" head nod.

I really don't know what happened next. After the first needle went into my face, right below my lower lip on my left side, I blacked out. I guess the electric shocks must have spread to my brain and my brain decided to close up shop for the evening.

When I woke up, I raised my head and looked cross-eyed down toward my chin to see the twenty thousand needles in my face. I looked like I had gotten into a fight with a porcupine and the porcupine had won! Adam had left the room, and any reminders of what just happened were gone from his little shop of horrors.

It was as though he needed to wipe the room clean and get rid of all the evidence. The candles were still burning, and there was a timer set for twenty-five minutes ticking down beside me, as well as what looked to be a cigar.

Every time I would move, I would get a little shock from all the needles throughout my body, so the only choice I had was to lie perfectly still for twenty-five, now twenty-four minutes.

Do you know how hard it is to be still and lie on a table with needles in you for, now, twenty-three minutes without freaking out? I did my best to calm myself, but it was hard to focus on my breathing when every time I exhaled, I was shocked by a needle. I felt my panic attack rising in my chest and at any moment I was going to lose it. Then another problem, an even bigger problem than a panic attack, arose. I had to go to the bathroom. Like really go to the bathroom.

This is what happens in my life. When I get stressed or anxious about something, inevitably in the near future, I have to go to the bathroom. This would be fine under normal circumstances, but what does a person do when dressed like a porcupine and they are having a bout of diarrhea?

I tried to call for Adam, but I couldn't due to the needles in my face. I thought if maybe I remained still on the table and rubbed my stomach the feeling would subside. How does one rub their stomach when their hands look like someone has thrown darts, in the form of needles, at their hands and fingers for about two hours? I might as well have been in a straitjacket because I had no use of my extremities, and I now knew exactly what a straitjacket felt like. I began to feel sorry for anyone who had had to wear such a ridiculous, tortuous outfit.

There was no other choice but to get off the table and hobble to the bathroom. I tried to slide off the table while keeping my legs as straight as possible so I did not pop off any needles.

Crap! One just popped off. Crap, there went another one when I took a step. Oh geez, there's another, and another.

This was my inner dialogue, as I couldn't speak anything out loud. My lips were basically glued shut because the needles were having the same effect. What is the horror flick where their mouths suddenly zip up? This was me! I didn't want to lose any of those needles in my face because, come hell or high water, I wasn't having those put back in! I was doing my best to scoot across the floor so I didn't dislodge the needles on my toes and feet. I managed to open the door with my stapled hands, and I noticed the coast was clear. The good news was I had a straight shot to the bathroom.

Getting to the bathroom was the easy part; using the bathroom without bending my legs was another problem altogether. I started off trying to do the hover maneuver, but I really had to go to the bathroom. The stress of figuring out how exactly I was going to do this just made the need to go even worse.

I finally gave in and sat down on the toilet. At that very moment, my legs sounded like the candy Pop Rocks when they go off in your mouth. All of the millions of needles that were strategically placed on my toes, feet, calves, knees, and thighs popped off and ricocheted off the wall—or the floor, I can't be certain. It was like a drive-by happening in the bathroom. I didn't care. It hurt so much, but at least I finally got to go to the bathroom!

I did the best I could to gather up all the debris from the bathroom floor. It looked like a murder scene because some of the places on my toes, feet, and legs had started to bleed, causing blood to drip on the floor. I hobbled back toward the room, and when I opened the door, Adam was there, and he didn't look like his normal chill self.

"What the heck happened? Where did you go?"

"Sorry, bro, I had to go to the bathroom. It was non-negotiable."

I handed him what was left of the needles on my lower body, or all that I could gather from the scene, and lay back on the table.

"Well, I'm not sure if the treatment has worked if those popped off before the timer went off. Do you know how long they were in before you went to the restroom?"

"I have no idea. I had to focus and work so hard to get to the bathroom before it was too late that the last thing on my mind was keeping the needles in on my lower half."

"Oh man, it was that bad, huh? Okay, let me take out the rest of the needles and we'll call it a day."

"I think that's a good course of action there, Adam, especially given all that we have been through today."

"Well, at least you didn't get sick to your stomach. Can you imagine having to hurl with those needles in your face? And why did you call me Adam?"

I had no answer. My acupuncturist just used the word "hurl," and I just might hurl if I didn't get away from the blueberry-smelling candles. Ten minutes later, after I had thanked Adam and said my goodbyes, as we would never meet again, the receptionist handed me my credit card and receipt.

"Gavin only charged you for half of the session since he said you had some, well, issues."

Issues...yes, I certainly had some issues for sure.

"Well, that was very kind of him. Thank you and have a nice life."

I took my credit card and receipt and hobbled out of the lobby. When I sat down in my car and looked in the mirror, I couldn't help but laugh. Bruises along my jawline had already begun to form and I thought, *Charlie was right!* He'd thrown in the towel two days ago, and I should have followed suit. I was now officially waving the white flag of surrender, and I was completely done with all medical treatments for my pain issues. As soon as I came to this conclusion, there was a knock on my window. It was the receptionist who I had told to have a nice life.

"Hey, Ginny, Gavin wanted me to tell you that you will probably be sore after this treatment, and you might consider taking two Advil and rubbing this on the areas that he treated."

She handed me a tube of Bengay, and with that, she was gone from my life forever.

Chapter 10

Bestie

After spending some time reading my diet and workout failure logs, as well as a phone call from my doctor regarding my latest lab work, the suggestion has been made that I need to make a tough, life-altering change. I have to say goodbye to my best friend.

When I mention I have to say goodbye to my best friend, I'm not referring to an actual human being. No, I'm referring to something far better—sugar. The white grains of crystal-like sand that make everything in life better.

I love her more than life itself. She is the essence of my being. I'm not sure how I can go on without her. I enjoy spending time with her in the mornings in the form of a donut covered with beautiful rainbow sprinkles. I love her as I sip my vanilla latte with whipped cream and caramel syrup on top. I enjoy having lunch with her when she is dressed up as simple carbs like fried chicken, crinkly French fries, and buttered toast washed down with a large ice-cold Dr Pepper.

She is my favorite snack when she presents herself to me as my afternoon Snickers candy bar. My evenings would not be complete without her company as I drown my sorrows in my high-carb pasta with breadsticks and a margarita on the rocks to accompany my meal. She is there for me in the middle of the night when I can't sleep, dressed as Nutella chocolate spread over my graham cracker, topped with marshmallows.

I even love her multiple personalities: Splenda, Extra, Sweet-n-Low, high-fructose corn syrup, sucrose, glucose, and aspartame to name a few. She is all around me. She makes my life complete, yet I have been told I must dissolve our friendship because she is poisonous to my health. How could something so wonderful be so toxic?

My doctor thinks I can just quit her cold turkey. He gives me no medicine or advice on how to proceed, just a "suck it up, buttercup" attitude.

"Dr. Edgemon, heroin addicts get orange juice and chocolate to help with their withdrawals. What are you going to give me to fight my sugar cravings, heroin?"

He doesn't find this amusing even after I explain what will happen. I'm such a sugar addict that if I do this cold turkey, I will be curled up in a ball with the shakes, and if a friend or family member saw me, they might say, "Heroin or meth withdrawal?" I would scream back at them, "No! Donuts, candy, cake, and Raising Cane's Chicken withdrawals." He still doesn't see the correlation.

On a side note, to my family and friends, if I die during this sugar withdrawal phase, please cremate me and spread my ashes over...Cane's—my favorite place on earth. This idea came to me while listening to the soundtrack of A Star Is Born. When Lady Gaga's character says to Bradley Cooper's character, "I don't feel this way about anyone else," this epiphany came to me—this is how I feel about Cane's Chicken.

Now that we have broken up, I am debating on whether I should change my status on Facebook. Is it too early? Would she be hurt by this sudden announcement? How much time is appropriate when you are dealing with forty years of being together? I mean, we spent a lifetime together, so should there be a grace period before I move forward?

Maybe we shouldn't have broken up? Should I take her back? Would she take me back after this bold move that I have made? Should I get visitation rights and see her on the weekend? I think maybe on the weekend and one day during the week. However, the week is long, so maybe a MWF and on-the-weekends scenario...what do you think? Yes, I agree that is what I should do. To hell with my doctor's recommendation!

Today I'll get back together with the love of my life, sugar. Sugar has always been there for me when others have let me down. We all put high expectations on our relationships, and many times the people in our lives let us down and fail to meet these expectations, but not sugar. She has always risen to any occasion and has never failed me. Many people will confess to being a dog or cat person, but not me; I am a sugar person.

I choose this wonderful entity over the human race. We have so many memories together that I just can't leave her behind. I can't decide which form I will dive into for our coming-back-together party. Should it be breakfast, lunch, snack, or dinner? All four? Yes,

I agree it should be all four. I mean, go big or go home! My life is back on track since I have my better half back in the picture. We'll celebrate our forty-year anniversary with donuts, fried chicken, cupcakes, and lots of Dr Pepper!

Chapter 11

Doogie Howser with a Laser

I have given you a glimpse of my not-so-super-healthy lifestyle by a sample of my daily diet, weenie-like exercise routine, and my obsession with sugar. You can probably imagine that my skin doesn't look so great based on my non-existent super-antioxidant diet. Instead of changing my diet and fixing my skin internally, I decided to just get a high-power laser treatment. It was a simple decision. On one hand, I could change my diet, eat whole grains, lean meats, veggies, and fruit, and cut out sugar (and all things awesome), or I could just zap my face with the laser...I will take the zapping!

The idea of this laser treatment was to zap all the brown, patchy sunspots on my face. They would eventually peel off, and my skin would be left looking like a baby's bottom. Well, let's just say that's not what happened!

I was escorted into my appointment by a very friendly nurse who seemed to like her job. She sat me down and we went through the usual: symptoms, prescriptions, menstrual cycle, blood pressure, and finally, she asked me to step on the scale.

"Do I have to get my weight just to have a laser treatment?"

"Yes, it's part of the standard protocol I must go through."

I sat back down on the table, already feeling defeated before the process began since I had to weigh, and she advised me to undress and put on the gown that was crumbled up beside me.

"I'm just doing my face, not my body. Is the gown necessary?"

"Yes, it's part of the standard protocol I must go through."

Geez, she was quite the stickler. I was guessing that she never cut off a tag on a mattress or stole a grape from the grocery store.

She left the room and I got undressed and put on the gown. I hate doctor's office gowns. They never fully cover you, and I can never figure out how to completely fasten them. The holes, those are so daunting. Once at a gyno visit, I put my head through the armhole because I was so nervous about seeing the doctor—those appointments are the worst. After I finished putting together a somewhat resemblance of what the gown was supposed to look like, the door opened, and the doctor and his sidekick walked in.

"Hello, Ms. Andrews. My name is Dr. Simpson, and this is my resident assistant, Dr. Atkins. He'll be assisting me today, and I understand we're doing an IPL treatment for the melasma on your face. Is this correct?"

"I don't know anything about the initials you just used for the name of the laser or what you called the dirt patches on my face, but yes, I want those gone and I was told you have the laser treatment to do it."

Dr. Simpson began an oration on the medical terminology for the patches on my face: what caused them, how to treat them, how the laser treatment would work, aftercare, and what I could expect from my treatments. The entire time he was talking, his sidekick never said a word. He just politely nodded after everything Dr. Simpson said as though he were a puppet or a battery-operated robot. When he was finished, he said it was nice to meet me and that Dr. Atkins would be doing my treatment.

I could feel a panic attack starting to creep in. I wanted to protest and say that I wanted Dr. Simpson to do the treatment, as that was the reason I came to a medical office and not a spa in the first place. I wanted to say, "Can you do the treatment and he watch? That sounds like assisting to me, not completely leaving the room, and having him do it. That's not assisting. That's taking over!"

Before I could put my thoughts into words, he left the room, and I was left with the puppet smiling at me like the cat who ate the family goldfish. He walked over to the laser machine, turned it on, and handed me some goggles. He told me I had to wear the goggles during the treatment to protect my eyes and that he would be wearing a pair as well. He went over everything that Dr. Simpson had already gone over, advised me to sit on the edge of the table, and told me he would start with my forehead and work his way down to my chin.

"The laser will feel like I'm popping you all over with rubber bands. We'll start at a low level and see how your face tolerates it, and then I'll bump it up gradually. The higher we go, the more successful the treatment will be. Do you have any questions?"

"No, I'm ready to begin."

He started to zap me, and it felt more like fifty rubber bands popping me at one time. He asked me after each zap how I was doing, and this only made it worse. I told him I was a big girl and could take it and he could just go to town. Well, he took the "go to town" speech seriously, and he began zapping me at a speed as fast as the Flash. I was gripping the sides of the table, and I began to smell burned hair, and we were still only on my forehead. I wasn't sure how I was going to make it through the rest of my face.

He paused for a moment, but the stop gave me no relief, as my face was on fire. I began to feel phantom zaps on my forehead although he had stopped. It was like when you were a kid and you went to the water park and spent five hours in the wave pool, and after you came home, you still felt the waves for another two hours. I was experiencing this, only in the form of zaps and not waves. I missed the waves. They were much more comforting.

"I'm going turn up the power a bit so that we can really get the patches on your cheeks and chin. Are you doing okay? Do you think you can handle it?"

No, I am not doing okay. I want to burst into tears and crawl back into the womb.

That's what I said in my head. However, I never back down from a challenge of any kind no matter how painful it is, and I couldn't let Doogie see my weakness. I nodded my head and gave him the thumbs-up to continue. I guess my courage gave him a jolt of adrenaline because he came back with vengeance. I wasn't dealing with the Flash anymore; he was more like the Joker because he had a demonic, crazy-like look in his eyes.

"I think this higher power is really going to get rid of your melasma. Hang tight, we're almost done."

I didn't hear any of that. All I could see was the drawn-on smile, white-painted face, and crazy flying green hair; all I could hear was his crazy high-pitched laugh as he was using his weapon on me. Finally, the zapping stopped, or I passed out (not sure what happened first), and he turned off the machine and removed our goggles.

"We're finished, and your face looks great. The patches are gone. Let me get you a mirror so you can see."

He handed me a mirror and I gasped out loud.

"Holy shit! What did you do to my face? I look like a fire engine and there's a hole on the right side of my hairline and a chunk missing from my right eyebrow!"

"Oh, uh, well the laser is supposed to make you red for a bit, and you had a brown patch by your hairline and eyebrow."

I think I would have chosen to keep the brown patch if it meant I got to keep my hair and my freaking eyebrow! You passed your MCAT to get into medical school, you are two years short of having a medical degree, and you chose to get the brown spot over saving my hair and eyebrow? A person who has fried their brain on drugs would have been smart enough to make a better decision there!

This was my Walter Mitty moment, as I said that in my head and not out loud. If I said it aloud, it would have been followed by nine hundred apologies. Even with a missing eyebrow and chunk from my hairline, I would still apologize—it's a problem.

"I'm very concerned with what I see here," is what I said back to him as I pointed to my hairline and eyebrow.

"Oh, I'm sorry. Don't worry—it will grow back. I've used the laser to treat my armpit hair, and it has taken six treatments to get it to not grow back, so I know your hair will grow back after one treatment."

That was wrong on so many levels. I sure hoped the laser was thoroughly cleaned before it went from his armpit to my face. Speaking of my face, it was not only redder than a tomato, it was now really beginning to sting.

"Do you have any cream to put on my face to stop the stinging?"

"No, most clients don't have pain afterward or redness."

"What? You just said redness was common as well as the stinging."

"Well, some redness and some stinging, but I've never seen anyone react the way you have."

I didn't have a response to his comment. I was rendered speechless. He told me when I got home, I could put some baby oil on it to stop the stinging and that the redness would subside, turn brown, and then begin to peel off. He left the room, and I got dressed, faster than the Flash, and headed to the front desk to check out.

The receptionist's back was facing me while she was on the phone. When she hung up, she spun around in her chair and gasped.

"Sorry, you startled me. Hello, ma'am. Let me check you out."

We both knew it was my face that startled her!

"What exactly did you have done?"

She wouldn't make eye contact with me, nor would the other receptionist, nor my rule-following nurse who had just walked up. They were staring at me, but only through side glances, and no direct eye contact. I told the receptionist what I had done, paid, and bolted for the door.

I could hear the chatter as I left. Every stop I made on my way home prompted the same initial response from people. I had several awkward, look-at-the-floor-and-avoid-eye-contact encounters. I was too scared to look at my face when I got home, so I applied the baby oil in the dark.

This all transpired on a Friday afternoon, and sadly by Monday, my face looked even scarier. However, I had to go to work, and work meant standing in front of high school students. All the kids in the school that were frequently bullied absolutely loved me because I gave them a break from being a constant target. I was now the target. It was like having a bull's eye on my face. I wanted to hold up a sign while standing in the hall that said, "I know, and I don't want to talk about it. It's hurting me a lot more than it's hurting you."

The red had now turned to a darker shade, a maroon, and it was as though I painted my face with maroon paint. I looked like Kelly Kapowski from *Saved by the Bell* when she used Zack's homemade zit cream, and it turned her face maroon. However, I couldn't pull the look off as well as Tiffani-Amber Thiessen did, that's for sure!

About a month later, my face finally cleared up, but it didn't look like a baby's bottom, and after one monthly cycle, my brown patches came back. At least the red/maroon cast had faded. I didn't hold a grudge against Doogie Howser, but I am afraid I can't call him

Doogie. You see Doogie was young and inexperienced, but he was good. Doogie would have never worked over my face the way the puppet did. In fact, I would have probably had a better outcome if Neil Patrick Harris had done my treatment. He would have at least sung show tunes while he was zapping me, and quite possibly there would have been dancing, and perhaps a magic trick or two.

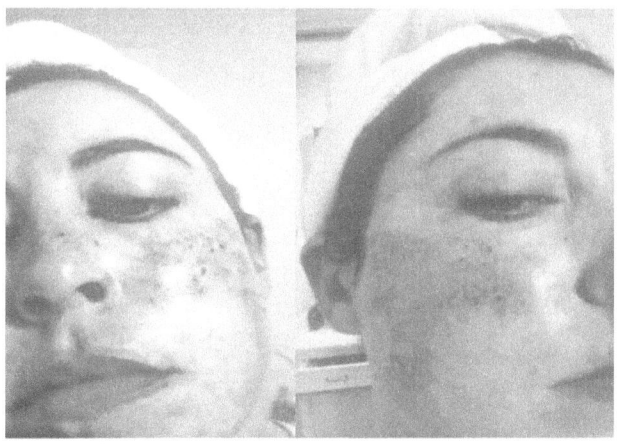

After the really bad laser treatment decision!

Chapter 12

Nanny for Hire

Why anyone would want to care for children as their full-time job perplexes me. My hat goes off to these people, and I have much admiration for them; I just can't do it. I had my first experience with nannyhood when I was around twenty-two. I was living in a big city and working four jobs to pay the rent. Being a nanny twice a week for a wealthy family with a two-year-old who was full of energy and tantrums happened to be one of the four ever-so-exciting gigs.

I'm the youngest in my family, so having two older brothers didn't render much experience in childcare. Growing up I did babysit a time or two for family and friends, but these kids were well out of diapers, and I was never asked to return.

I saw the ad for a nanny on the Innerweb, and the hours and pay were exactly what I was looking for—aside from having to care for a kid from dawn until dusk. This same internet site was also where my best friend found her psychopath roommate who is now in jail. It just makes sense that as a parent you would find your child's nanny in this same spot.

I responded to the ad, and I was immediately contacted by the mother. We met at a restaurant near her house, and she brought along the job, I mean kid, so the two of us could meet. We hit it off well, or well enough for me to get the job, and I was hired on the spot and asked to start the following week.

If I were a small child and my mother had hired my caretaker in a local pub after this person had responded to an ad on the Internet, I would have found a way to turn my mother in to Child Protective Services. I know that my references weren't checked prior to our meeting or after I was hired because, being the nosy person that I am, I called and followed up on this fact. I guess she hired me in good faith because I have a trustworthy face, but then again, so do most serial killers.

The first day on the job, I arrived at 8:00 a.m. sharp. My car rolled into the driveway of a fancy red brick home surrounded by other luxurious houses. I received hateful looks from the neighbors and joggers because my exhaust pipe leaked smoke all the way up the drive. I might as well have had a sign on the outside of my car that said, "I'm not from around here." The mother showed me around the house, took me through her son's routine, and gave me a list of do's and don'ts. She said her two older kids would be home by 4:00 p.m., but they would take care of themselves when they arrived, and my sole responsibility was Junior.

Around 8:30 a.m. Junior started making noise on the monitor, and I knew this shit was about to get real. She reintroduced us and then went into her office and shut the door. The major problem was that she worked from home, and her office was across the hall from Junior's room. This made for a real problem when he got upset with me and wanted to see his mother but she was on a conference call.

This particular predicament brought on my first experience with the infamous two-year-old tantrum. I had honestly never experienced this type of psychotic breakdown. Junior started screaming and throwing his body on the floor. I'd seen something similar the night before in a cheesy horror flick. At any minute, I expected his head to start spinning and for his voice to change into a demonic tone. I ran over to him and tried to comfort him, but he kept shouting, "No," and he started swatting at me. About two minutes later he fell down, and I rushed over to pick him up as he lay lifeless on the ground. I called for his mom because I was sure he was ill or had something medically wrong with him to exhibit such behavior.

She came out of her office, gingerly stepped over his body, and said, "Nah, he's okay, he just had a tantrum. It's best just to ignore him when he goes through one."

Every alarm in my head went off, and I thought to myself, *This is a normal thing, and it will be reoccurring? Why in the heck didn't you post that in the details of your ad?*

After the tantrum passed, I had to frantically get lunch together because he was supposed to eat at the same time every day so that he could be put down for his nap at the same time every day, and we couldn't deviate from the schedule. As I prepared his lunch and was about to heat it up in the microwave, his mother walked in and said, "Oh, don't heat his food up on the plastic plate because plastic heated in the microwave can cause cancer. Also, please make sure he eats all his vegetables so that he'll have three very good bowel movements today."

Thirty minutes later, I was in his room changing one of his three daily bowel movements. He didn't just have a bowel movement. This kid dropped explosive poop bombs that filled up his diaper and oozed out the sides. Guess who had to defuse these bombs? Yours truly!

After he awoke from his naps, we would go to the park or to music class. These two events required me to drive him, and this was something that even my parents frowned upon. They knew that every time I got behind the wheel it was detrimental to the other drivers on the road and me!

On rare occasions, I would pop by McDonald's and pick me up some food after we finished with the ever-exciting music class. I always felt bad when I got something and left Junior to eat his vegetables and organic fruit. In a moment of weakness, I got him a Happy Meal and told him not to tell mommy about our "special meal." The family that I worked for was vegan and only ate organic food.

Being vegan is like eating cardboard—wait, you must make sure that the cardboard is made from organic, recycled material, otherwise, you can't eat it. Sometimes I would just crave greasy, dangerously bad-for-you food and felt that Junior needed to have this experience too, as well as the nifty toy that came with the heart attack. As soon as we walked in the door from music class, Junior said, "Mommy, look what I got in my Happy Meal!" I was scolded for feeding him fast food. Afterward I think she made him go on a specialized cleanse made for little people that was given to them by their kooky pediatrician.

The pinnacle of my nanny gig occurred about six months after I started and involved swimming lessons. Junior was starting swimming lessons with another kid in the neighborhood. We arrived at the scene fully prepared in our swim diaper and Snoopy swim trunks. Before he hit the water, I greased him down from head to toe with sunscreen.

He was so slick that when I tried to put on his floaties they slid right off! The swim instructor, who looked like Richard Simmons's brother, informed me that this was big boy swimming lessons, and we didn't need our floaties. He motioned for the boys to come over and get in the water, and Bobby, Junior's friend, jumped right into the pool. The swim instructor screamed, "Good job, Bobby, what a big boy!"

The swim instructor looked over in our direction, and Junior started shaking his head and yelling his favorite word, "No," repeatedly. I knew we were on the verge of another tantrum, so I thought I would help things out a bit. I squatted down to his level and said, "Hey, Junior, the water is fun, and Bobby is waiting for you to come and play with him."

"No, I don't want to. I hate swimming lessons!"

I am so glad that your mother made us come if you hate swimming.

After twenty minutes of coaxing Junior into the water, we were as successful as the Dallas Cowboys in any of their playoff runs in the last twenty years. Finally, after everyone was completely frustrated, I decided to accidentally push him in the water. This isn't as bad as it sounds. I mean, it wasn't as though no one else was in the pool, and I knew once he was in that the swim instructor would grab him and he would love it! I contemplated this endeavor for about ten minutes as I tried to convince him to slowly walk into the water one step at a time.

When I had no success, I decided to go for it. I reached over and gently lifted him up and heaved him toward the swim instructor. He made a big splash, and I started yelling, "Good job, Junior. See? I told you it would be fun!" He began to scream at the top of his lungs, and he started flailing his arms and legs. The swim instructor gave me a "go to hell look" and handed Junior over to me.

Bobby's mom came running over with Junior's mom (oh boy), and they both demanded to know what happened. The swim instructor informed them I had thrown Junior into the pool. I tried to explain that I didn't throw him into the pool and the theory I had behind it, but neither mother would listen to me.

He told the two mothers what I did could cause Junior some major psychological problems; he would probably have a fear of water for the rest of his life. He was really going for the theatrical effect here. I was asked to leave the house and to never come back, and Junior's mom hurled my check at me as I was shoved out the door.

My gig as a nanny was short-lived and was ended by a Richard Simmons lookalike who sported a way-too-tight light pink speedo. I should have known he would be trouble. Nevertheless, I guess it was for the best, and I don't hold any of this against Richard. I had mad respect for him. Under different circumstances, he and I could be great friends. I had potentially given Junior cancer, as I forgot several times and heated his plastic plate in the microwave.

I might have caused him to have a heart condition with the two Happy Meals from McDonald's. Finally, I caused him to have a fear of swimming pools and water in general for the rest of his life. It was probably best that I didn't give him anymore complexes. My heart goes out to his next nanny, and I hope this person can handle his explosive diapers, temper tantrums, and his newfound fear of water.

Best of luck to you,

Ginny

Chapter 13

Jesus Took the Wheel

W e don't have good luck with vehicles in my family. My dad is a farmer, and the inside of his truck looks like a goat lives in it on a daily basis. For Father's Day, my brothers and I gave Dad a year's worth of once-a-week car washes. A buddy of mine from high school had a mobile wash, and he gave us a good deal. Even better, he would come to my parents' house every Sunday and wash it on-site. It seemed like a good idea at the time, and for the first two months, we had no issues.

One afternoon Rob came to their house and asked if he could take my dad's truck to his shop to wash it. He said he was out of some of his supplies, but he had them stored at his shop. My dad didn't think anything of it and gladly gave him his keys, and Rob said he would have his truck back by 4:00 that afternoon. By 6:00, my dad didn't have his truck, and Rob wouldn't answer his phone. Around 8:00 that evening, my dad got a phone call from Rob's mom, Suzy. Dad told her that Rob had taken his truck to his shop to wash, but he hadn't seen or heard from him since 2:00, and his truck was MIA.

Suzy informed my dad that Rob didn't have a shop, and she had received some weird phone calls from him and was terribly worried. Being the patient man that he is, my dad decided to wait it out overnight, and the next day around noon Suzy and her boyfriend showed up at my parents' house.

"Mr. Andrews, my son has been messing around with some 'bad medicine,' and the phone calls he has made to me make him sound like he's on another planet."

Apparently, Rob was driving my dad's truck on this so-called planet.

My dad decided he had to call the police, mainly for Rob's safety, but he also needed his truck back. It was hard to take the bus to the farm. A policeman came over to the house and asked the necessary questions to file the report. He told my dad they would handle it and to just wait it out.

Although my dad is a patient man, he is not so great at playing the waiting game in certain situations. He once had rotator cuff surgery, and two days later he was building a fence on the farm and couldn't understand why the doctor was mad at him. It had been a week, and there was no news from the police. We had several friends call us to give us "Rob spottings" in the area but no solid leads. I even tried to reach out to Rob on Facebook. I sent him several messages letting him know that we cared about him and that no one was upset, but we needed the truck back.

Bus fares out to the country were getting expensive. I never heard back from him, and after another week had passed, the farmer was getting restless. My parents went out one night for dinner, and as they were driving home my dad yelled, "Stop! There's my truck and Rob's driving it."

My mom spun the car around and they began to chase Rob down. I guess during the high-speed chase my dad managed to call the police officer who had been assigned to his case.

"Mr. Andrews, please turn the car around and go home, and we'll take care of it."

"Like hell, you will. It's been two weeks, and you've come up with nothing. Now my wife and I are hot on his trail. Try and catch up!"

My dad—aka Dominic Toretto—managed to make another call during his car escapade that was straight out of the movie *The Fast and the Furious*, and that call was to my brother.

My brother immediately called me. "Gin, we have a serious issue. Mom and Dad are in a high-speed chase after Rob, and they're in Mom's car. Mom's driving with Dad yelling at her to stay on his tail."

"Oh boy. So, you are telling me the streets of our small West Texas town are in danger by a 1982 Toyota Camry driven by an enraged woman being motivated by an outraged farmer in his late sixties out for vengeance on the man who stole his goat truck?"

"Yep, that's right," my brother stated while laughing.

"Should we help?" I asked out of concern.

"Nah, I think I'll pop some popcorn, go over to their house, turn on the news, and watch it as it happens. Want to come over?"

I replied, "Sure, I'm on my way. Pop the Butter Lovers and not the Butter Light. The light version tastes horrible and gives me the runs."

About an hour later, my parents arrived home with only one vehicle. The Toyota Camry was now overheated, and they were completely exhausted. They both looked like they had just run a marathon.

"Man, that is hard work trying to keep up such high speeds while following someone," my mom said as she sank into her chair. "My shoulders, neck, and knuckles are sore. I'm not cut out for a life of crime or crime fighting."

My dad followed her into the living room, and as he sank down in his recliner, he uttered some curse words under his breath. Just as they were about to settle down and relax, the doorbell rang. It turned out to be the cop and his partner who had been assigned to the case. They asked us to step outside on the porch while they searched the house.

"Dad, who and what exactly are they looking for in the house? I'm pretty sure Rob isn't in there since you just saw him on Loop 982, and if he were here, your truck would be in the driveway, unless he took a cab."

"Ginny, pipe down. I'm not in the mood."

When we were allowed back into the house, we found our dog, Lady, lying on her back in front of the stairs with her paws up. I think she was saying, "Don't shoot, don't shoot, but even I know Rob isn't here, you idiots. Now would you mind rubbing my belly?"

The police advised my dad to sit tight and not to engage in any more high-speed chases after Rob, and if we spotted or heard from him to give them a call immediately. My dad closed and locked the door and plopped back down in his chair, but this time with a beer in hand. Two hours later, my dad received a phone call from the police informing him that they had his truck. If he could come up to Rosa's Mexican Restaurant off Loop 982, they would gladly turn it over to him.

My family made the news twice that night. Once at 6:00 p.m. for the Vin Diesel car chase, and again at 10:00 p.m. for the strange vehicle occurrence at Rosa's Mexican Restaurant off Loop 982. When my dad and brother arrived at the scene to pick up his truck, the officer hadn't prepared him for what he would find. His front bumper was almost completely torn off and it was hanging on the ground. It was barely attached to the truck by a couple of remaining pieces that were still intact. The windshield was cracked in four places, there were several dents on the hood and side of the truck, and the back bumper was smashed in four oddly spaced-out places. Rob was smiling at my dad while he was being handcuffed and put into the back of the police car.

"What the hell happened to my truck?"

"Well, you see, Mr. Andrews, when we finally caught up with Rob, he was at the hospital downtown doing wheelies in the parking lot. We chased him into a corner and thought we had him, but then he drove down the stairs in front of the hospital and escaped out the other end."

"How did he end up here and what's with the crop circles to the left of the restaurant?"

"Well, uh, that's how we caught him. He was doing circles in this lot beside the restaurant. We were able to stop him and get him out of the vehicle."

"What did he say when he got out of the truck?"

"He said he was Jesus. He was advised to make a crop circle so that the UFO that was picking him up knew where to land."

My dad just shook his head and didn't know what to say.

"Your truck smells bad, and there are a ton of black spots and soot from the extracurricular activities that went on in there. He must have taken in a lot to get him to the point where he thought he was Jesus waiting on a UFO to land...if you catch my drift."

My dad grabbed his keys, and he and my brother climbed into the truck and were grateful when it started.

My brother turned to my dad, laughed, and said, "Well, I guess Jesus really did take the wheel!"

My dad didn't get the Carrie Underwood song reference, and he popped my brother in the back of the head and told him never to speak of this incident again. The truck came to a screeching halt as they pulled up to the collision shop.

My dad placed the keys inside the drop box, and he cursed under his breath because he knew he would have to continue to take the bus to the farm for another two weeks or more. It gave a whole new meaning to the saying, "Built Ford Tough."

Chapter 14

Resale Value

I got nervous today. I mean really nervous. My friend bought a brand-new Louis Vuitton handbag, what I like to call a purse, and she carried it today without Scotch Guarding it beforehand. I mean, does she know the serious risk she's taking? Does she know that just one small stain on that thing could damage its resale value? How can people live so dangerously?

Everything in my life is for sale and has a dollar amount attached to it. Here's the drill when I purchase something new: I buy the product and Scotchgard it, if possible. I leave the plastic cover over several areas, if possible.

Did you know that you can leave the plastic cover over most items and this will help protect them from marks and scratches that would potentially affect the resale value? Now if you choose to go this route, many people will say to you, "Ma'am, there's a plastic cover on the side of your purse." Just smile and ignore them, as you are living life the correct way: safe, secure, and protecting resale value at all times.

The next step is to make sure to keep and store the box, tags, and packing material. When I do finally decide to wear it (after carefully weighing the pros and cons while using a t-chart to make sure I don't want to return it), I wear it with the utmost caution. This way when I am ready to resell it, I can clean it up and place it in its original box. I keep the plastic string used to latch on the tags, and I carefully retie them onto the item. After all this work, the item looks brand-new, and we are open for business!

My favorite thing to resell is a car. I tend to trade out cars as often as most women trade out handbags. On a side note, why are they called handbags? They really aren't bags for your hand because you use your forearm, elbow, or shoulder to carry them. Bags you carry in your hand are called clutches or wristlets, and the latter is for your wrist. A clutch is the only "handbag" for your hand. Cars have clutches...so you see, purses and cars have a lot in common, besides both having great resale value!

Car buying, selling, and trading is an addiction, and I can't seem to stop myself. Some people have binge eating sessions or will go on shopping sprees and return the clothes, both of which I have done frequently; however, I soon moved into the car-buying category.

It began with a 2005 Nissan Altima. This was my very first real car purchase as an adult. I kept that one for almost two years before my car-buying binge sessions began. I traded in my Altima for a shiny red Nissan Frontier Nismo truck. I was new to the car-buying process, and my salesman wasn't the nicest.

I kept trying to knock him lower and lower on the price to get my trade difference lower since my Altima didn't have quite as much resale value as I had hoped. He finally got irritated and turned his computer around to me and declared, "One hundred bucks is all I will make on this sale, so I can assure you a trade difference of six thousand is the best I can do."

I looked over at the corner of his desk and saw a picture of Emilio Estevez and him at a BMW charity event. I guess he thought he was super cool since he was buds with E.E. and he didn't have time to waste on the commission he would make on my pitiful sale. I imagined myself ten years down the road walking into the dealership with E.E. and the two of us are about to buy a super expensive, brand-new car from our new salesman. However, before we seal the deal, I look over at my salesman from the past and pull a Julia Roberts in *Pretty Woman*: "'Big mistake, big, huge.' E.E. and I will take two of the cars on display. I'll have a silver one, and he'll have a black one."

Sadly, I was sent back to reality when he asked me how I would like to pay for the truck, and I remembered that I was a high school teacher who was about to write a check for the biggest amount she had ever written, $6,000. I had to remind myself how to write a check, and one for that amount, and to be honest, I wasn't sure I did it correctly.

We finished all the documents and then he handed me the two sets of keys. He basically shoved me out of his office to greet a more affluent client who was waiting on him. I didn't care how he treated me. All that mattered was that I was now the proud owner of "Big Red," and he had a huge amount of resale value. I peeled out in the parking lot as I sped away! Well, not exactly. Peeling out would throw up rocks, and that would cause paint chips and have a major impact on Big Red's resale value.

My first mistake of my car binging run was trading Big Red for a Honda Accord that smelled like an ashtray regardless of the seven fog treatments the dealership claimed to have done to make it smoke-free. A very poor decision on my part, as smoke is a definite no-no when it comes to resale. I got hosed on this deal. Even though it wasn't my first rodeo, I acted like a complete rookie in the deal and let the dealership rob me of my shiny, red truck, and I was left with Smokey.

Since Smokey, the number of cars I have sold, traded, and purchased is far too many for me to keep up with. They were all an attempt to get back the money I lost on Big Red. I would buy a used car and then try to flip it. Most people are in the house flipping business, but I was making a run at the car flipping business and crashing. I finally realized that I could never get back the money I had lost and Big Red was forever gone—a lesson to learn. A very hard lesson to learn, and one I would always be reminded of every time I saw a red truck pass me on the road.

I sold a lot of cars during those five years, but I made sure to stick to the three-per-year rule to avoid the IRS and having to get my dealer's license. My family told me I should get my dealer's license and open "Ginny's Autos," but secretly I knew that business venture would cause me to have to file for bankruptcy.

I was losing money instead of making money. My resales didn't have much sale to them. My friends would tease me and tell me that everything in my life was for sale. Too bad I couldn't string up my cars along the inside lining of my jacket, but then where would I put my gold chains?

I guess flipping houses is better than flipping cars. Cars can't really be flipped too successfully. Bottom line is I took a big loss when I traded in Big Red, and I will never overcome this loss unless I win the lottery. Big Red, I miss you, wherever you are.

I hope your new owner appreciates your resale value better than I did. I should have known you had a good amount of worth when I discovered you had a remote that operated your stereo. How could I have been such an idiot? I guess some things in life really are not for resale!

Chapter 15

Alanis Morissette

When a person goes through a tough time in their life, they usually rely on God, friends, family, a significant other, and perhaps Oprah and her couch. Just like Ricky Bobby, played by the amazing Will Ferrell, said in *Talladega Nights*, "Help me, Oprah Winfrey!" All these options are excellent choices; although, during my tough times, I find myself turning to my girl, Alanis.

This extraordinary, rocking-out lady speaks to my soul. It's like she's in my head and private thoughts daily. However, I am not sure of the proper way to pronounce her name. I say A-lan-is, but that's because I'm from Texas. I'm sure the proper pronunciation is Ah-lawn-nis. No matter how you say it—she's been my idol since I was a freshman in high school, and we are still going strong! These are some classic lines from her songs that have kept me going through the years:

"Eight Easy Steps"

"*How to keep smiling when you're thinking of killing yourself.*"

I think every teacher can relate to this. You walk through the halls with a smile on your face, and your interactions with staff and students are much like Dory from *Finding Nemo* but your inner dialogue is as dark as Deadpool.

As a first-year teacher, your boss tells you two days before school starts that you will have to teach a sex education unit as part of your health class. You give her a Dory smile and just keep swimming; meanwhile, your inner Deadpool says, *Like a sex ed class will do these homies any good. They already get more action than half of the teachers in the school!*

Mason, who is a habitual liar, has given you a million reasons why he doesn't have his essay ready in your college-level class, and this has happened all semester long. You take a deep breath in as he starts a batch of more excuses: "I swear I had it ready! I submitted it online, but as soon as I hit submit our power went out. I would have brought you a hard copy, but I don't have a printer. I can't show you the proof on my laptop because my dad took it on a work trip." You respond with a Dory smile and tell him to get it to you ASAP;

meanwhile, Deadpool is wreaking havoc on your inner dialogue. *This kid should really think about laying off the pot. Next time he starts in on his excuses I'll have to light up a doobie—maybe he can share his!*

When your coworker asks you to watch her class during your only conference period, Dory smiles and says, "I'm happy to...no, I promise...I don't mind at all." Deadpool thinks, *I have got to find another job that doesn't require me to cover for other people when they aren't doing their jobs!*

"You Learn"

"You live, you learn..."

There is so much truth to the chorus of this song. You live, you learn...a new lesson every day, and the great Alanis covers all moments: in love, tears, losing, bleeding, screaming, grieving, laughing, choosing, praying, asking, all the things!

I learned this morning that it's really hard to put a pair of ballet tights on another person, particularly if that person is four and moving around a lot. Even worse is when you discover the tights are "too tight," and you can't get them past her thighs. However, you worked so hard that you tell her she can wear low-waisted tights to dance. She rocked those sagging, gangster tights like no other four-year-old ballerina would. When you love, you learn—that love can hurt and when your four-year-old niece comes out of ballet and she has been scolded by the teacher for her tights, she screams at you, "I don't like you, Aunt Ginny." This hurts, and then you cry and learn to skip the tights next time.

When you lose, you learn—that you suck and your opponent is better than you, at least on that day.

When you bleed, you learn—if it's a lot of blood, you better go to the hospital or you will die, and while they treat you at the hospital, you scream.

When the dog dies, you grieve, and you learn—to never get another one because you never want to feel that level of hurt again.

When you choke, you learn—that if you don't get a kind soul to give you the Heimlich maneuver in a correct and timely manner you will die. This is a constant fear for a single person who lives alone. Like, who will be my Heimlich man?

When you laugh, you learn—that laughter is the only way to get through the tough times, but don't laugh too hard because as you get older you will pee. Just wait for it; it's coming.

When you choose, you learn—that sometimes you make the wrong choice, and some choices you will learn from for the rest of your life.

When you pray, you learn—that sometimes you get an immediate answer and other times you don't get an answer at all. You then feel like a chicken running around with its head cut off in a dark, dark room.

When you ask questions, you learn—unless it's in my family. In my family, my questions are met with, "Ginny, I've already answered that question a hundred times, and I will not answer it again."

No matter what happens in the end, there are always new lessons to learn. An hour ago, I learned you can't put foil in the microwave, but it can go in the oven. I must have gotten those two rules mixed up, as my food exploded in the microwave, and I think the machine is now broken. It's okay because you live, you learn. I have learned that no matter what I am going through, I can turn on an Alanis song and she makes everything so much better!

I would like to end this chapter with a nod to the great Ms. Morissette. I combined her "Hand in My Pocket" song with the everyday challenges of being a teacher. Alanis—please don't sue me. Now, DJ, drop that beat.

I'm broke 'cause I teach school
I'm poor 'cause I chose the wrong field
I'm stressed and I'm grouchy—yeah!
I'm lost and not hopeful
I'm underpaid and overworked
I binge on the food in the teachers' lounge...
help me!

And what it all comes down to
Is that everything is gonna be fine, fine, fine
'Cause I got one hand in my pocket, and the
other is waiting for Christmas!

I'm drunk while on the job
I'm checked out but still have bills to pay
I'm old and super tired—yeah!
I don't want to cover a sub shortage
I care but you've sucked the life from me

I'm done with waste of time in-services,
thank you!

And what it all comes down to
Is that everything is gonna be fine, fine, fine
'Cause I got one hand in my pocket, and the
other is waiting for spring break!

And what it all comes down to
Is that I got it all figured out right now—
I need to quit!
'Cause I got one hand on my keyboard
Searching up jobs on Indeed!

Kids are on their phones
Failure rates are off the charts
Inmates run the prison—yeah!
My lunch is only twenty minutes
Pay raises and bonuses don't exist
Coach down the hall shows movies on same
pay scale...help me!

And what it all comes down to
Is that everything is gonna be fine, fine, fine
'Cause I got one hand in my pocket, and the
other is waiting for summer!

And what it all comes down to, my teacher
friends, yeah
Is that everything is gonna be fine, fine, fine
'Cause I got two hands on my keyboard,
typing my resignation letter!

Chapter 16

I Am a Donkey

Everyone has a spirit animal. I could tell you mine is a butterfly because I am going through a period of major change and I will come out transformed, but that would be a lie; mine is really a hamster. A hamster on a wheel to be precise—a huge metaphor for my life. In all areas of my life, I feel like I'm working super, super hard, but alas, I am just like that hamster on the wheel—I'm going nowhere!

Or maybe my spirit animal is closer to a donkey because lately, I feel more like a jackass than a hamster. The proper name for a female donkey is a "jenny," which happens to be a version of my own name, just spelled a little differently. The gals can also be called she-asses. Your average person refers to all donkeys, male and female, as jackasses—even though the jack is reserved for the male. I really felt the need to break this down for you. Also, the research is legit. I found it all on Google.

Therefore, I am a version of a donkey. A jenny-ass, she-ass, or a jackass used incorrectly—I am all the things. This is only fitting seeing as how many of my behaviors always provoke the word "jackass" to come out of the mouths of innocent bystanders who witness my disastrous actions.

I'm never dressed appropriately for any occasion, I always say the wrong thing at the wrong time, and bad luck follows me around like that hemorrhoid you can't seem to get rid of, like ever. Funerals and weddings happen to be my favorite venue for living up to my name. I don't mean to be disrespectful or inappropriate; it just happens.

I think I come by this naturally, as I was taught to be awkward at an early age at funerals. When I was a child, I witnessed my cousin walking into a family funeral, and he taped a "get well soon" balloon on the casket. No one said anything to him, and everyone acted like that was something a normal-acting forty-five-year-old man would do.

Weddings are tough gigs for me. It is extremely hard for me to stay focused, be serious, and not engage in or cause a laughing spell. I have been a bridesmaid, like fifty times, and during one of my stints, my friends (I was acquainted with both the bride and groom) decided to write their own lyrics, I mean vows. At one point the bride said, "I will be your cheerleader for life," and the groom replied by saying, "I will be the team captain of this family, and it will be the A team."

What if they had a son that hated sports and wouldn't even make the C team? What if the daughter was a stoner and hated cheerleaders? I tried to hold my breath, bite my tongue, anything to keep from laughing. Simultaneously, I looked over at another bridesmaid and saw her struggling to hold it in, we made eye contact, and then I lost it. My covered-up laugh came out like a snort, and then I coughed to cover it up—then it turned into a case of the body shakes, and even the preacher stopped and stared at me.

During another run as a bridesmaid, I was using one of the portable potties at the reception (note to self: Don't have a reception outside where women who are dressed up must squat on portable potties; this is a difficult task in a pair of shorts, let alone an evening gown), and I fell over, and the portable potty went with me. Luckily, we weren't on a hill, but it was enough commotion to draw a crowd, and this all transpired while the bride and groom were having their first dance.

I thought those apparatuses were secure enough not to be pushed over. However, the task of setting them up was given to one of the cousins, and he didn't secure them to the ground properly. When I was set back upright, I opened the door to be greeted by half of the wedding reception, including the photographer, who snapped a couple of pictures. I'm positive that one made the wedding album!

*The ass is missing his ass in the picture
because I hired a cheap photographer!*

Maybe I do all the above so-called "jackass" moves because sometimes my mind just doesn't function properly, like at all. Sometimes my mind decides to go on a vacation, and it forgets to inform the rest of my body. I once burned my backside and lady parts on a heating pad because I fell asleep. I must move around when I sleep because the pad was placed securely on my lower back to start. I frequently get my foot tangled in the sheets and come to work with a bruise on my face on a regular basis. I believe my neighbor teacher suspects abuse, but the abuse is coming solely from me.

My most recent bout of stupidity occurred while I was flying from Texas to California. I really try to decrease water intake when I'm flying due to having a fear of using the facilities on a plane. This fear probably stems from my aforementioned roll in the hay as a bridesmaid. Basically, on that night I got into a fight with the portable potty and the potty won. Maybe it's the fear of the plane going down while I'm stuck on the pot. My eulogy would read, "She died while doing what she loved..." Using the bathroom?

I try to avoid using the bathroom on a plane at all costs. As much preparation as I put into not having to go to the bathroom, the unthinkable happened—I had to pee and there was no holding it.

I unfastened my seatbelt and made sure the light for the bathroom showed to be unoccupied. I looked around to make sure there wasn't anyone else wanting to use the facilities to avoid the awkward, "No, you go first, no, it's okay you were here first" talk. The coast was clear.

Luckily, I was sitting in an aisle seat, and I made a mad dash to the front of the plane. Houston, we have a problem! When I got up to the front of the plane, I couldn't find the bathroom. I assumed it was located directly below the sign, but the only thing remotely resembling a bathroom directly below the sign was a tiny storage cabinet. I know this because I opened it. This is where they store the oxygen masks and inflatable yellow vests.

I ventured farther up to the front, and what I thought was the bathroom was the cockpit. I soon realized I was starting to cause a scene, and several of the passengers in the front of the plane were staring at me. Meanwhile, I still needed to pee, and if we hit a bout of turbulence, this would happen without the use of the facilities.

My snoop session caused stress to the passengers because someone buzzed a flight attendant to come to the front.

"Excuse me, ma'am, but what exactly are you doing up here?"

On a side note, I really hate the word ma'am now that I'm older. It makes me feel my age, and I would rather someone say the F word to me than ma'am.

"Hah, well this is embarrassing, but I'm trying to find the bathroom."

He began to point and give me a tour of the journey I had just taken around the front of the plane. "Well, your first stop was our storage closet, and next was the cockpit. Did you actually think the bathroom was in the closet?"

Oh man, I already felt like "my name," and he was making matters so much worse by getting the attention of everyone in the front of the plane. The last straw was that he was being snarky to add to the stress. I had to do something. I had to defend my jackass status, or at least try.

"Hah, yes, I guess I had one too many drinks, and I'm a little disoriented. If you would kindly show me where the restroom is, I would appreciate it."

"Well, it's to your left, but during your tour, someone else slipped in there. You'll have to go back to your seat and wait because there's no gathering at the front of the plane."

I turned around and headed back to my seat feeling defeated, and my bladder now hurt from still needing to pee. The truth of the matter is I didn't have any alcoholic beverages; I had to lie to cover up my embarrassing tour of the plane in lieu of trying to find the bathroom. I was also mad that I didn't have the guts to tell the flight attendant off and take up for myself.

This is the story of my life. I never take up for myself because, as stated at the start of this book, I hate confrontation. While growing up, my friends would have the courage to tell off the school bully, but when I told her off, I ended up telling her I liked her hair and nails.

I went back to my seat, and I sat there fuming over the fact that I was a coward—worse, a coward that was about to get a UTI! I waited about five minutes and then saw that the bathroom was now free. I unfastened my seatbelt, gave myself a pep talk, and started to get up.

"Attention, everyone, this is your captain speaking. We are about to experience some heavy turbulence, so I am going to ask that everyone remain seated for the remainder of the flight."

Some people were put on this planet to be geniuses. They will excel in academics, publish papers, create inventions, and pee on planes with no trouble at all. I'm not this type of person. Meanwhile, I frequently go through fast food drive-thru windows and forget to order at the speaker. When I pull up to the window, I get scolded for not ordering my food beforehand. The sad thing is I have done this about ten times. I guess

I should just embrace the struggle and be thankful for the adventures and stories that go along with the journey, but I'm not quite there.

I am currently driving down the access road looking for the frontage road. I've driven twenty miles, and I still haven't seen a sign that says "Frontage." The nice lady at the gas station twenty miles back told me to take a right on the frontage road, go several miles, and then my destination would be on the left side of the freeway.

Oh well, the scenery is very beautiful out here with lots of cows, horses, and cotton. I'm not sure why they would have cotton and livestock so close to a freeway, but I guess that's life in the big city. I sure hope I find the frontage road soon because I really need to pee.

Again, with the missing body parts—guess you have to pay extra for full coverage!

Chapter 17

All Things Awkward

Andrews is awkward. This is an understatement. I have come to accept this fact, and I believe I was born this way. You would think as time goes on, this would get better; however, the older I get, the worse this quirk gets! Change plays a major role in the level of awkwardness.

I hate change as much as I hate confrontation. There should be a class required of all teenagers after they hit puberty (which ruined my life, by the way) that teaches all of us how to deal with change. Change in general, but more importantly, change with our bodies.

You overcome puberty, and rock the teenage years and your twenties, but then things start to go south in your thirties. I'm in my forties, and the other day I noticed my ass is now running into my legs—like when did this happen, and why wasn't I warned about this from a class or textbook in school?

Beyond the awkwardness that happens with an aging body, my everyday occurrences go south—quite fast. My awkward flag flies high when I'm around men that I find attractive.

I was graciously giving my time to help my cousin's baseball team with a fundraising event. We were running a snow-cone-hotdog-health-department-will-soon-shut-us-down stand at one of the softball tournaments in town. All I had to do was serve up the supplies because I wasn't allowed to do any cooking. Fine by me! One of the really good-looking (like Zoolander material) single dads approached our stand, and the awkwardness inside me began to rise.

"Hi, Jason, can I get you anything?"

"Hi, Ginny, I don't really like hotdogs, but I'll buy a hotdog from you."

"I would eat your hotdog. Wait, I don't want to eat it, like it's your hotdog, but I'm glad you're inviting me to play with your hotdog. Oh man, that sounded bad. I didn't mean it like that." The whole time I was rambling my face was turning fifty shades of...red.

Meanwhile, back in normal-ville, the mom helping me, who has two kids on the team, was staring at me and pissed that I got inappropriate in front of her two kids. I didn't mean to; it's the awkwardness inside me that goes dirty south.

A couple of weeks later, I was out with a group of friends, and we were enjoying a good time at a wine bar. I'm always hungry, so I ordered a meat and cheese tray for the group, and things got crazy when the waiter delivered it.

"Who ordered the meat and cheese tray and where should I put it?"

"I did, and you can put your meat right here."

I didn't think anything about it, and I just smiled right back at the hot-looking male waiter; however, when I glanced around the room, I was met with shock and awe. Much like when I look into the mirror these days.

Since I have a ton of awkward moments in a day, this leads me to apologize a lot! Like a lot! Plus, I'm OCD, so apologizing for people like me is the same as breathing and wearing deodorant for others. If my apology doesn't go well, then I apologize again, and then I apologize for apologizing too much. This really aggravates my family and friends.

Maybe it's a gender thing as well. At least with the people I'm around, women tend to apologize more than men, and their apologies are very different. A woman apologizing for cheating on her boyfriend would go something like this:

"I'm so sorry. I don't know what's wrong with me. This is all me, not you. Can you ever forgive me?" Two weeks later: "I'm so sorry. How can I make this up to you?" One month later: "Will you ever forgive me? We can go to therapy to work through this!" Four months later, even after therapy, she is still apologizing.

Take the man in this same scenario. "I'm so sorry I slept with your best friend; my package just slipped in." One apology, final answer. He doesn't want to phone a friend and isn't allowed to phone that friend ever again.

One of my most significant awkward moments, that did indeed require an apology afterward, happened when I attended an event for my best friend's daughter. I grew up in a small town, and I loved that small town—greatest upbringing ever, but we didn't do a lot of fancy things like the big city girls did. When my friend, Melissa, asked me to attend her daughter's

Assembly Club event, my first thought was, *What are we assembling?*

I was given specific instructions regarding my dress. Apparently, my low-key, dress-for-comfort attire embarrassed even my friends. Melissa advised me to dress to impress, and I told her that would be a problem because I don't attend any event in which I can't wear elastic pants. But since she's my good friend, I decided to make an exception. I threw on my nicest Jessica Simpson dress and heels from DSW, and I headed to the shindig.

When I arrived, Melissa told me to meet her in the dressing room. As I strolled back to the VIP lounge, I was in a state of shock. Was her daughter getting married? Like, a surprise, on-the-spot wedding? That's cool. I mean, she's only sixteen but hey, maybe this is a new trend. Glancing around the room, I saw other girls in wedding dresses...were they getting married too? Hopefully not to the same groom. More importantly, twenty-five sixteen-year-olds were beating my old ass to the altar!

Melissa could tell I was perplexed, and she said, "This is MaryBeth's 'welcome to society' party."

I shook my head and said, "Wasn't her welcome to society party the day she came out of your vagina?"

This comment was followed by tons of shaming and degrading looks cast my way and lots of apologies on my end. In fact, I'm still apologizing to my friend Melissa, and her daughter, to this day.

Although that was a rough night, the appetizers were rocking, and I got some great ideas for future wedding dress designs. All things come together in the end—but when they don't, you still get some delicious potato skins and queso.

Chapter 18

False Advertising

Telemarketers are getting really savvy and smart, and now they're using local numbers when they call. I end up thinking it's my doctor or some important call and I answer. Today I didn't answer, and they left a voicemail.

"It has been brought to our attention that the warranty on your car has expired. Please give us a call and have your credit card info ready. We can set you up with an extended factory warranty for far less than what the dealership would charge you."

If I were allowed to speak to them, I would have responded with, "Of course the original warranty on my car has expired. I drive a 2004 Toyota Corolla!"

Facebook is another form of false advertising. You know those games on Facebook that are meant to usually cheer you up? I clicked on one that said, "Why are you single?" I was thinking it would say something like, "Ginny, you're single because you have devoted your whole life to your career." Or "Ginny, you're single because you just haven't found Mr. Right. Hang in there, love is around the corner." Nope, I got, "Ginny, you're single because you're an asshole!" Wow, thanks, Facebook.

Why are you single?

Ginny, you are single because...

You are such an asshole.

Also, the ten-year challenge on Facebook only helps those in their twenties. It's cute to compare your ten-year-old self to your twenty-year-old self, but anyone thirty and above...it doesn't fare well for us. For the love of all that is holy and just in this world, don't do it!

Who wore it best challenge. My thirty-year-old self did because the forty-year-old self can't fit in it! Compare the two pictures game, what is the difference between the two? Well, in this picture there are wrinkles above the forehead, around the mouth and eyes. Picture two doesn't have any wrinkles. This challenge turns into a seek and find on my face. Find the big wrinkle beside her mouth and circle it, find the forehead wrinkles—find the saggy skin under her eyes for bonus points!

All this to say, I am very leery of advertising. Like do you actually think when you donate to ASPCA, after seeing the Sarah McLachlan commercial and donating all of your money or pleading to adopt fifteen dogs, that your money is actually going to help the dog on the screen and the other animals?

Or does it all go to some random guy living in his parents' basement? Is it all a hoax? I don't care if it is. I'll still donate every time I see that commercial, and PETA/ASPCA, don't come after me—I fully support you and the animals. I guess I'm just skeptical.

This terrible, negative attitude stems from being burned. Shortly after the Sarah McLachlan commercial, a preacher came on selling holy water that heals, and he looked legit. In my defense, he had a cross necklace, Bible in his hands, the whole nine yards. I called the number, got the water, and my body still feels like a ninety-year-old. It's as though my entire body is encased in an armored suit of bubble wrap because it pops like a machine gun when I wake up. I sure wish I could get that $140 back!

The biggest scam happened to me in person. A health clinic near my house was offering Covid aftercare. It clearly stated this on the jumbotron outside of their office, or maybe that's called a marquee...who knows. I walked up to the receptionist, Sheryl, who hated life and her job, and I said, "I'm here for the Covid aftercare treatment."

She replied, "We don't offer that."

There was another sign advertising Covid aftercare directly to my left; I could see it in my peripheral vision. I did the "look at sign, look at her, look at sign, look at her" move, but she still didn't get it.

Next, I asked her, "Have you ever seen the movie *Three Amigos?*"

"Yes."

"You know the scene when Steve Martin is on top of a building and he's trying to get the amigos below to see him without getting caught?"

She just stared back at me with no words even attempted.

"Remember when he goes, 'Hey, guys—look up here, look up here, look up here! You two, look up here, look up here, look up here!'" Then I pointed to her sign and said, "Look at me, look at me, look at me!" All said in a very high-pitched, bird-like voice.

Sheryl, without cracking a smile, said, "We don't make those signs, and it's an old one."

"Okay. Is your sign guy here?"

"No."

"Well, can you get a message to him? Tell the oracle, aka the sign guy, to make a new sign because he's creating false hope and crushing dreams. You're in the healthcare business. You're supposed to provide care and instill hope in your patients."

"Do you want to see the doctor?"

"Well, I guess since I can't get Covid aftercare I'll see him for this random rash on the side of my neck. Do I get a discount for the false advertising?"

"No."

"Well shit, Sheryl."

Chapter 19

Party for One

I am blessed with the best—the best friends and family anyone could ask for, but sometimes I have to give them a break from my weirdness. Some days I feel like saying to my friends, "Sorry, I can't hang out right now. I'm watching the *Tomb Raider* movies (all of them, Angie and Alicia) while wearing a braid and eating Little Debbie cakes. I hope they inspire me to change my diet and workout."

It takes me far longer than anyone I know to figure things out. Life can be hard. Furthermore, figuring out the questions to my biggest concerns can be even more difficult: what is my purpose, who am I, and what do I want out of life?

More importantly, how did Halle Berry's dog that was shot in *John Wick 3* suddenly show up and start attacking men's balls? Like, did the vest protect him and we just didn't see that scene? And why do those movies always involve dogs getting killed or hurt?

Musical theater is another concept I struggle with. I have mad respect for actors who can master this art. I can't sing at all—I wish I could. I tried out for a play in college and didn't realize I would have to sing as part of the audition. Even after telling the directors, I wasn't going for a singing part, they insisted it was all a part of the process.

I belted out "Amazing Grace" (that's the only song I know verbatim) and needless to say, no grace was extended my way. What I can't fathom is how do theater actors sing in each other's faces without laughing or spitting? The musicals where they sing every line, like, no dialogue in between songs, just all song, I can't get into. Just tell him you don't love him and run off; singing it makes it so much harder and draws it out!

The interactive musical theater productions where they put the actors in the aisles to make it more real and collaborative—I like this, but what if you have to go to the bathroom or need a snack? Then you run into the actor and ruin the show. I have done this several times.

My last attempt at a musical was *Jekyll and Hyde*, and I left in a complete state of confusion. Why is Hyde the bad guy? Dr. Henry Jekyll sounds like a mafia boss or serial killer; Mr. Edward Hyde sounds like a successful businessman or professor. I respectfully disagree with the name choices. I don't like how it ends with him just dying and that's it...how about he dies, but his fiancée finds love or carries on his research? I need more! But I also went to the bathroom and got some Cheez-Its around this time, successfully avoiding any actors in the aisle, so maybe there was more to the ending of the musical.

I get a constant reminder of my inability to figure things out as quickly as most when I hear the Challenger School ads on Pandora when I'm working out. I gather that school is for very gifted and talented kiddos—like Mensa kids. I like the ad where they give an example of the second-grade class reading *Charlotte's Web*. The teacher asks, "How would you compare Charlotte to Wilbur?" The seven-year-old child says, "I would rather have a self-reliant friend because they would want to earn things and work for them versus just having things given to them."

Geez, I don't even know what self-reliant means. If I were in that class and asked that question, I would be like, "I like Charlotte better because she's nice, but then they're both nice, so I don't really know. That's a hard question. Do I have time to make a t-chart for comparison?"

During my lady time of the month, my brain disappears, and it's vital that I give my friends and family a break from my brain and grouchiness. I have a constant dialogue of, "It's not you guys, it's me. Well, more like my uterus—it's like Ted Bundy, while my mind and heart are like Betty White."

I end up complaining a ton and have a terrible attitude. I just want to make an announcement during this time of the month that says, "My right ovary hurts. Like, men don't have days where they say, 'My right ball hurts,' unless someone kicks them there. No one punched me in the ovary; it just hurts. Being a woman sucks sometimes!"

My niece and I like to go to the movies, and I think it's incredible the amount of knowledge and life lessons they're putting into kid movies these days. They're tackling the tough issues—even the female stuff. I remember when I was growing up, all you got was a super awkward talk from your mom, and then she would show up to school with your pads. There was no hip, coming-of-age movie to go see with your friends beforehand. Well, that isn't entirely true. There was

My Girl, but that caused more issues than it helped. Not only did you leave that movie having a fear of getting your period—you also feared bees and your best friend dying.

The movie *Turning Red* was more helpful to me than my ten-year-old niece. Meilin, I can relate with your mom waving pads on school grounds! Although Meilin doesn't get her period, instead she turns into a giant red panda whenever she gets emotional. I would like this option, please. Let me be a cute, cuddly, popular, money-making red panda, versus acting out metamorphosis scenes from the musical *Jekyll and Hyde*. I too can relate, as my mind and heart fight my uterus for a solid week, much like Jekyll fights Hyde. Red panda for the win.

A second popular movie that helps educate kids on the tough lessons in life is *Encanto*. I have trouble pronouncing that one, though. I say Encanta, {E}ncognito, {E}ncontinence...we don't talk about peeing ourselves, because it happens when you get older. Then you must borrow pads from Meilin's mom. Both are great movies; I loved *Encanto*. I'm finally pronouncing it right, but my ten-year-old niece and my friend who is a second-grade teacher did a better job of summing up the life lessons that lie within.

One of my favorite memories as a kid was driving home after seeing a movie with my dad and having him break down the literary elements and relate them to my life. Those moments are priceless, and I always try to do the same with my niece. However, she usually ends up saying, "Aunt Ginny, can we table this conversation until you've re-watched the movie and have a better grasp on it and go get a corndog at Sonic instead?" Corndogs make great memories too!

Chapter 20

Answers to Life's Biggest Questions

Y **es, Please.**

In Amy Poehler's amazing book, Yes Please, she says, "I like to say, 'Yes, please' as an answer to a lot of things in my personal and professional life."

I agree with the awesome Amy Poehler regarding the phrase "yes, please." She talks about why it's a good phrase to use, which scenarios could present occasions to use the phrase as a proper response, and why she chose this phrase as the title of her book. I too feel like many questions or statements in life can be answered with, "Yes, please." Here are some scenarios I have noticed in my own life.

Most items on paperwork that you fill out can be answered like so:

Sex. "Yes, please."

Income. "Yes, please."

Married. "Yes, please."

When you drive up to any fast-food restaurant and they ask if you want the larger size of their menu item, a simple, "Yes, please," will suffice.

I think the world might be a better place if we answered most questions with this response. When the homeless man on the corner asks you for some money, you can respond with, "Yes, please...gladly accept this twenty-dollar bill." Every time a charity organization calls your house asking for donations you could respond with, "Yes, please...send me the information and I will get a check in the mail tomorrow."

I know this isn't a new concept. In the movie *Yes Man*, Jim Carrey plays a character who must say yes to everything that comes his way. By the end of the movie, he realizes he can't say yes to everything, as it causes problems. Bad example...I forgot about the ending to this movie, and that totally negates my "yes, please" scenario.

Yes, But

I changed my mind. Maybe the answer should be "Yes, but" instead of "Yes, please." For example, items on paperwork that you fill out can be answered like so:

Sex. "Yes, but can I pick my partner...?"

Income. "Yes, but can I be paid in cash?"

Married. "Yes, but not for long."

When you drive up to any fast-food restaurant and they ask if you want the larger size of their menu item, a simple, "Yes, but can you make the fries the smaller size, as I am watching my weight?" will suffice.

I think the world might be a better place if we answered most questions with this response. When the homeless man on the corner asks you for some money, you can respond with, "Yes, but buy the six-pack of beer and not the twelve-pack so you can buy food as well." Every time a charity organization calls your house asking for donations, you could respond with, "Yes, but I can only send twenty-five dollars right now, as times are tough for me as well."

Yes, And

I changed my mind. Maybe the answer should be "Yes, and" instead of "Yes, but." For example, items on paperwork that you fill out can be answered like so:

Sex. "Yes, and can we get takeout?"

Income. "Yes, and can I be paid in large bills?"

Married. "Yes, and divorced."

When you drive up to any fast-food restaurant and they ask if you want the larger size of their menu item, a simple, "Yes, and can you throw in an apple pie?" will suffice.

I think the world might be a better place if we answered most questions with this response. When the homeless man on the corner asks you for some money, you can respond with, "Yes, and maybe buy the two-pack this time so you can buy enough food for two meals." Every time a charity organization calls your house asking for donations, you could respond with, "Yes, and please accept just fifteen this go as times are even tougher."

Yes and No

I changed my mind. Maybe the answer should be "Yes and no" instead of "Yes, and." Sometimes you need the best of both worlds. For example, most items on paperwork that you fill out can be answered like so:

Sex. "Yes at first and no because it's not fun anymore."

Income. "Yes at first and no, now I am all sold out."

Married. "Yes, I was, and no, I will never be again."

When you drive up to any fast-food restaurant and they ask if you want the larger size of their menu item, a simple, "Yes, I would love to...oh no, I forgot I can't! Due to all the upsizing, my body is now upsizing, and I can't button my pants."

I think the world might be a better place if we answered most questions with this response. When the homeless man on the corner asks you for some money, you can respond with, "Yes, and no, please don't buy the two-pack. Maybe just get yourself a single and spend the rest on lots of food." Every time a charity organization calls your house asking for donations, you could respond with, "Yes, that is a great idea for those who you are helping out, and no has to be my answer, as it's not a good idea for me at this time. You see, times are tougher than the last time we talked."

No

I changed my mind. Maybe the answer should just be "No." Sometimes you must protect yourself and keep it simple. For example, most items on paperwork that you fill out can be answered like so:

Sex. "No."

Income. "No."

Married. "No."

When you drive up to any fast-food restaurant and they ask if you want the larger size of their menu item, a simple "No" will suffice.

I think the world would be a better place if we answered most questions with this response. When the homeless man on the corner asks you for some money you can respond with, "No. As a matter of fact, I gave you so much that now I am homeless. It's okay, it's not your fault, and we can still be friends. Sorry if I was rude." Every time a charity organization calls your house asking for donations, you could respond with, "No." Then you could ask if it would it be possible to get on the list to receive their charity because you donated most of your income. Then say you are sorry. Sorry is always good.

Silence

I changed my mind. Maybe the answer should just be complete and utter silence. The world would be a better place if everyone just kept their mouth shut.

Chapter 21

"Good Talk...Good Talk"

T his seems to be my mantra lately. Almost every conversation, major event, or life circumstance for me recently could end with a simple, **"Good Talk...Good Talk."** This is a perfect way to end an awkward conversation or to soften the blow when you get bad news. It can also be used as a classic closing line when you aren't sure what exactly to say, but you feel you need to say something, rather than just stay silent or walk away. When I was a teacher and coach, I had many, many conversations that ended with this epic saying:

"Hello, Coach Andrews, this is Veronica's mom. I'm sorry to disturb you at home on the weekend, but I just wanted to call you and tell you that Veronica and her best friend don't like you, and they're about to quit the team. I also wanted to inform you that if you make her pick up trash one more time while she can't work out due to her acid reflux, I will be contacting your boss. It isn't my child's place or role to pick up trash, even if she polluted the area; it's the responsibility of the custodial staff of the school, not my child."

"Good Talk...Good Talk."

"Ms. Andrews, this is Robin Olsen, and my son, Barret, was looking to take your public speaking class this fall. You seem like a kind, understanding person and can imagine that many students have major anxiety when it comes to taking a public speaking course. Surely you can see this. With this being said, I was hoping you could understand Barret's issue and maybe make an exception when it comes to his giving speeches in front of the class. You see, he has some speech anxiety. I know your class is a college-level class, but could he be allowed to just write his speeches and read them silently to himself in front of you practicing his non-verbal communication skills? Would you allow this to count for his speech credit without having to give an actual speech? I appreciate your considering this option for him. By the way, my husband is Chip Olsen, and he's president of the school board. Thank you."

"Good Talk...Good Talk."

Not only have I had some pretty interesting conversations with parents, I have also had my fair share of classic teacher fails. Why is it that kids are never listening when you're going over something important, but they are all tuned in, front and center, when you have an epic failure in front of them?

While reading aloud to my students I came upon the word monotony and said, "MONO-TONY," because that's how it looks! I looked up to see if anyone noticed my giant flop, and of course, all my students were deadpan staring at me. I thought to myself, *You all had massive ADHD five minutes ago and were acting like you drank two Red Bulls and a Mountain Dew before you came to my class. Now, during my fail, you're all in!*

I said, "Tony, the one who sits in the back, yeah, he's out with mono. See what I did there? 'Mono-Tony.' It's fine, he'll be fine. He'll get to his goal weight, but he'll be fine. Keep him in your thoughts and send good vibes his way, but Tony will be back. Now let's get back to the excerpt we were reading."

"Good Talk...Good Talk."

At the start of the next semester, I had a new set of students. I was trying to establish a rapport with my class, and I realized they all liked working out. On a side note, I tend to mix up and make up words, and many times, I don't know the correct meaning of various words. I also tend to be as naïve and clueless as Ariel from *The Little Mermaid* when she first discovers the human world. For several classes in a row, we had been talking about workouts and nutrition here and there. One day in class I said, "I've been working out faithfully, but I'm just not seeing the gains."

One of my students said, "Ms. Andrews, if you want to get ripped, you have to eat a ton of protein, like your bodyweight in half. That's how much protein you must consume in a day."

I did the math in my head, and I was like, "Crap, I have to lose weight! That's way too much protein to consume. Do I just walk around with a piece of bacon in my mouth? How is it possible to get that much protein in one day?"

Then another student said, "Ms. Andrews, you can just do protein shakes and bars!"

And that's when it happened! I said, "Yeah, but those are good until you swallow, and then they leave a wang in your mouth!"

It wasn't until later that night that I realized what I had done! As I watched *Deadpool* (always a classic movie after a rough day), I heard him say, "I'm just gonna hang out with my wang out!" Shit! In that moment, I realized the damage! I didn't get the memo that wang was a slang term for penis! Like, who knew? Well, apparently everyone did!

The word I needed to use was twang...maybe? More importantly, I just said, "It's good until you swallow, and it leaves a wang in your mouth," in front of hormonal high school boys and girls. It now makes sense why the room went silent! But what about the song, "Everybody have fun tonight...everybody Wang Chung tonight?" What kind of wang are they chunging? I don't understand!

"Good Talk...Good Talk."

Shortly after that debacle, we started having major vandalism in the bathrooms. Below is the motivational pep talk I gave my students to get them to stop.

"Students, it's time to get real. I've watched this go on all year long and we must talk about it so it can get better for next year. This whole vandalism in the bathrooms isn't helping anyone. Especially me, when I need to pee, and the pot is missing! Then I need to wash my hands—nope, the soap dispenser is missing, and you can forget about the paper towels, those homies have been gone since the second day of school."

I stopped to see if they were listening before I charged on. "Girls, your vandalism is super positive! Like, don't keep doing it, but way to go on the positive side. You have cheerful, uplifting remarks written on the mirrors, hotline help info on the walls, and in place of the paper towel dispenser, you have a Bible verse on a sticky note. Like, I don't even care that you stole the paper towel dispenser. You made up for it with the note. You repented!"

I turned to look at the boys in the room. "Boys, this is not the case. I don't go in the boys' restroom, but I get daily reports from Mr. Smith, the math teacher down the hall, regarding what's going on in that restroom. There are no uplifting notes on the mirror, no hotline help information, and no Bible verses. Instead, you're putting donuts in the urinals. What in the world would possess you to waste a good donut like that? Have you lost your mind?"

Then one student shouted out, "Ms. Andrews, it's bad in there. Five minutes ago, there was a giant-size peen-z on the wall."

I said, "Bob, I am afraid to ask, but what is a peen-z?"

"Ms. Andrews, you're a grown woman. Surely you know what a peen-z is."

"Bob, do you mean penis?"

"Yes, I do."

"Bob, can you wipe off the peen-z? Was it done in sharpie or expo?"

"Ms. Andrews, I am not touching or rubbing the peen-z."

"Okay, Bob, thanks for sharing."

"Good Talk...Good Talk."

Not only have I used that saying to try and "save face" after awkward moments while teaching, but I have also used it in my personal life quite a bit.

"Ms. Andrews, this is Josh Hinson, the lead fire marshal on your case. Is this a good time to call? Okay, well I pleaded your case with the insurance company and told them that when the lightning struck your house it damaged your hardwood floor, A/C unit, hot water heater, all electronics, and the foundation on the front of the house. However, they're still saying that the damages won't be covered by the specific insurance policy you have. I even threw in that it injured your cat, Arnie, for added sympathy, but it didn't help. Sorry, and I'm also sorry about Arnie. I'm glad he survived, but I'm sorry he is now cross-eyed and walks with a limp. Good luck to you and take care."

"Good Talk...Good Talk."

"Hi, Chris, how is your wife doing?"

"Well, Ginny, we got divorced two years ago after she cheated on me with my brother."

"Good Talk...Good Talk."

"Hi, Karen, you look so awesome. You have that baby glow about you."

"Ginny, I'm not pregnant, and screw you for adding to my stress level."

"Good Talk...Good Talk."

"Hey, Rick, is your girlfriend coming to dinner with us?"

"No, Ginny. We broke up after she decided she wanted to date girls."

"Good Talk...Good Talk."

"Phil, your baby girl is so cute. What's her name?"

"Ginny, that's my son, and his name is Zane."

"Good Talk...Good Talk."

"Hey, Coach Andrews, I thought that was you. I'm here waiting on my girlfriend to finish her appointment. You see, our baby girl is due in October. Are you pregnant too? Oh, my bad, sorry for my mistake, forgive me. I guess it's kind of awkward to run into one of your students, particularly a male student, at a gynecology doctor's appointment, but my girlfriend makes me come with her. Well, it was good to see you. I hope all goes well with your exam."

"Good Talk...Good Talk."

"Hey, Gin! Man, it's good to see you. This is my wife, Sunni. Hah, well, uh, I know when we were together, I said I wasn't ready to get married and didn't want children. I guess I changed because here I am, and we're five months pregnant! It was so great running into you."

"Good Talk...Good Talk."

In some of these scenarios, I dig myself into a hole so deep that someone needs a tractor, not a shovel, to pull me out; therefore, my only response can be:

"Good Talk...Good Talk."

The picture I have painted with my bad news and awkward scenarios is a bit dark, I know, but just because one has a bit of bad luck and some really awkward moments, it doesn't mean that life is all bad. I have learned to embrace my awkward, bad luck moments and accept my failures. I'm good at failing!

All of us are doing the best we can to navigate our ships through the sea of life. Every chance we get, we're doubling up on our life jackets (I like to wear three while at the lake), making sure our lifeboats are still intact and working, and feeling pretty good if our ship stays afloat!

Sometimes, "the best you can" means that you don't leave your house for a week so that you don't have to put on clothes or comb your hair.

Sometimes "the best you can" means you don't return any texts or phone calls for another week, and the only human interaction you have is with the kind people during your fast-food drive-thru raids.

During these raids, you remember to order first at the speaker before you pull up to the window to get your food!

You do what you must do to get through the tough times. You do you!

The tough times can, and usually do, make you stronger—but it may take several fast-food drive-thru raids to get you there. Stick with it and keep fighting the good fight. You can use my awkward and bad luck moments to keep you going, or you can listen to Alanis Morissette, because she will cure all your problems.

I guess what I'm trying to say is that everything will be okay one way or another.

So, suck it up, butter cup, and stay the course.

Even if you fall off the course and almost drown in the lake beside the course, it will be okay because in the end, we are all going to make it...somehow, some way.

"Good Talk...Good Talk!"

*Sometimes you just need to have a heart-to-heart talk with a donkey. Even if his ass is cut off and you are being photobombed by a jealous horse!

Acknowledgements

They say it takes a village to raise kids—well, it takes an entire entourage to help me adult! This book would not be possible without the love and support of so many people. First to thank is God...this is His work through me, and He knows I need a ton of help! God, sorry about the cuss words...I am a work in progress!

Now for the earthly support staff: first and foremost, to my parents, Rusty and Linda. I wouldn't be who I am today without your love and support, and I don't have the words to thank you enough. I would like to thank all my family—including my brothers, sisters-in-law, nieces, nephew, uncles, aunts, and cousins—for your love and support.

To my wonderful friends and comedy support staff: Holly Churchwell, Amanda Robles, Kristen Webb, Farron Yowell, Blair Thacker, Cilla Willis, Cody Burns, Becca Moss, Austin Griffin, Bonnie May Nichols, and

Laura Wilkes Patton—thank you for giving me a push and supporting my work. Also, thank you for putting up with me all these years! Dana Taylor and Jeanne Manning, thank you for being amazing mentors.

Melissa Waggoner, Jamie White, Ashley and Adelle Davis, Erica Palmer, McKaylie Campbell, Traci Wiseley, thank you for being my friends and putting up with me in our adult years...like really adult years!

Book support staff: Altah Swindle, Sue Vernon, Connie Pfanmiller, Elene Georgopoulos, and Buffy Rattan—thank you for being my friends and my first-round editors! To the FHS English teaching crew, the OGs and the new crop, you are the best! Thank you for your help and friendship.

Kimber Rodgers, Marcia Crabtree, and Morgan Vaughan—thank you for being amazing friends and beta readers. Thank you for believing in my work and pushing me. Lauren Brownell, Leslie Glenn, Deanna Tapley, Melissa Adams, and Sarah Ketchem—thank you for your guidance.

Hidie Henry and Kristen Tucker, thank you for your amazing photography skills—you didn't cut off images, that was my dad! Michael Khan, Belynda Brown, Danie Craig-Orozco, and Ashtyn Kahn at

UDawg Graphics—thank you for the help and amazing artwork! Danie, you are top notch!

Thank you to Tom and Sally McSpadden and Seeger. Jimmy and Leigh Anne Dunlap, Elvis, Marilyn, Bella, Bebe, and Maci for your canine support and facility use! Also, for providing gainful employment while writing!

Mark #1, Mark #2, Chris, Anna, Talley, and Robert...thank you for the legal tips. I left your last names off for protection so you won't be connected with me should things go south!

Audrey Mackaman, thank you for being an amazing editor. Christena Stephens, thank for being a rock star proofreader. I appreciate you both putting up with my insane amount of questions and checks! KJ Waters, this wouldn't have happened without you. Thank you for your patience, guidance, knowledge, and hard work. Lauren, thank you for connecting us. Jessie Andersen, you started it all—thank you!

To my former players, students, and coworkers at TCHS, MHS, FHS, NGC...thank you for your belief in me and the impact you had on my life.

Thank you to everyone who has supported Ginny Andrews Comedy. The comments, likes, and shares of my videos warm my heart and keep me motivated to keep on keeping on!

This section is for everyone I have forgotten. Thank you! Technically I didn't forget you—you go in this section. Thank you to Dutch Bros, Starbucks, Raising Cane's Chicken, Dr Pepper, and Little Debbie—you gave me the stamina to press on, and I love you!

Disclaimers

Disclaimer #1

Apparently, I mention a great deal of products and items in my book that require a trademark or copyright symbol. Originally, I had the symbols throughout my book; however, since I use so many (I drink a crapton of Dr Pepper), it became distracting to the reader. They are listed below and deserve great praise!

After reviewing the list, I realize I need to clean up my diet, but I should be good to go in the aches and pains category! Yes, you read that correctly—I said Chia Pet! Thank you to the good people who created the below products:

Vicks VapoRub, Desitin, Vaseline, Little Debbie, Doritos, Pibb Xtra, Dr Pepper, Bengay, Botox, Dasuquin, Vans, Chia Pet, Pop Rocks, Advil, Snickers,

Splenda, Extra, Sweet'n Low, Cheez-It, Facebook, Preparation H, Milk Duds, and Garcinia Cambogia.

These are some of the places that keep me living my best life:

CVS, Starbucks, Dutch Bros, Taco Bell, and Raising Cane's Chicken Fingers.

A special shout-out to Pandora Music, Challenger School ads, and any other places or products that were mentioned in my book that I may have failed to mention in this section.

Disclaimer #2

The chapter, "Answers to Life's Biggest Questions," was written about twelve years ago, and it has since undergone a face-lift. After I wrote it, I came across the awesome comedian Amy Poehler's, *Yes Please*[1], book. We can both agree that phrase can have a great deal of use and meaning in a person's life. I have cited her book below since I made references to it, and I highly encourage you to buy it. It is far better than mine! Maybe HarperCollins will pick my book up too. No, probably not, but it was worth putting it out there.

Disclaimer #3

I have been obsessed with Alanis Morissette since I was a freshman in high school. In the chapter, "Alanis Morissette," I make references to several of her incredible songs. Below are the citations to her songs, "Hand in My Pocket[2]" and "You Learn[3]" from the amazing album, *Jagged Little Pill*, and "Eight Easy Steps[4]" from the album *So-Called Chaos*. If you don't know who she is, or don't listen to her music, we can't be friends.

---

1. Poehler, A. (2014). Yes Please. HarperCollins Publishers.

2. Morissette, Alanis & Ballard, Glen. (1995). Hand in My Pocket [Song]. On Jagged Little Pill [Album]. Reprise Records and Maverick.

3. Morissette, Alanis & Ballard, Glen. (1995). You Learn [Song]. On Jagged Little Pill [Album]. Reprise Records and Maverick.

4. Morissette, Alanis. (2004). Eight Easy Steps [Song]. On So-Called Chaos [Album]. Maverick.

About the Author

Follow my ass:

GinnyAndrewsComedy.com

Instagram, Tik Tok, Twitter: @gindrews10

YouTube, Facebook: Ginny Andrews Comedy

*9 7 9 8 9 8 8 4 1 9 9 1 4 *